133268

289.30924
Hickman, W.
   Brigham's destroying angel

Dooly County Library
Lake Blackshear Regional Library
Vienna, Georgia 31092

Brigham's Destroying Angel

WILLIAM A. HICKMAN.

Brigham's Destroying Angel:

BEING THE

LIFE, CONFESSION, AND STARTLING DISCLOSURES

OF THE NOTORIOUS

BILL HICKMAN,

THE DANITE CHIEF OF UTAH.

Written by Himself, with Explanatory Notes by

J. H. BEADLE, ESQ.,

OF SALT LAKE CITY.

ILLUSTRATED.

BOOKS FOR LIBRARIES PRESS
FREEPORT, NEW YORK

DOOLY COUNTY LIBRARY
Vienna, Georgia

133268

First Published 1904
Reprinted 1971

INTERNATIONAL STANDARD BOOK NUMBER:
0-8369-5951-5

LIBRARY OF CONGRESS CATALOG CARD NUMBER:
74-165642

PRINTED IN THE UNITED STATES OF AMERICA

PREFACE.

It was in the Winter of 1868-9, that the editor first saw the subject of this work upon the street in Salt Lake. He was then spoken of generally in Utah as one of the notabilities of an epoch long past. I never heard him mentioned as having any connection with church or civil matters of recent occurrence. For years I had heard of "Bill Hickman, Chief of the Destroying Angels, Head Danite," &c., *ad nauseam;* but like most persons unacquainted with Mormon history, I regarded such matters as the creations of a fertile fancy. When convinced by a longer residence in Utah that there was and had long been *some* kind of a secret organization dangerous to Gentile and recusant Mormons. I began to examine the history of the Church more carefully; and while all the Mormon people spoke of Bill Hickman as a desperately bad man, and guilty of untold murders, I was struck by two curious and then unexplainable facts:—

1. The first was, that while everybody, from Brigham Young down, united in calling Hickman a murderer, and while evidence could easily be collected of several of his crimes, *not a single attempt had been made by priest or people to bring him to justice.* For twenty years the Mormons had the courts and juries exclusively in their own hands. During that time many persons had been executed for crime; they could do as they pleased in judicial matters, and abundant evidence was before them against Hickman; but no grand jury ever moved, there was no indictment, and not even a complaint before an examining magistrate. This indicated *something*—but what? Until I obtained Hickman's manuscript, I never fully knew. When Hickman was arrested all the Mormon speakers and papers united in denouncing him as "a notorious criminal, who had long been able to evade justice." If this was known, as they admit it was, why was not Hickman arrested and punished during that long period in which the Mormons arrested and punished whomsoever

they pleased? Ah, why, indeed—except upon the explanation given in this book.

2. The second point is, that long after Hickman was known as a murderer he was successively promoted to a number of offices; he was Sheriff and Representative of one county, Assessor and Collector of Taxes, and Marshal; and during all this time *he was on terms of personal intimacy with Brigham Young.* He was "in fellowship" in the Church until 1864, and Porter Rockwell, his compeer in crime, is a member of the Mormon Church in "full fellowship" to-day, and now the companion of Brigham Young in his travels! Can these things be explained on any theory, except that the statements in this book are true?

During all the changes of 1869 and '70 I rarely heard of Hickman. At length, in the autumn of 1870, while at Stockton, Utah, I heard the account of his polygamous wife, which is detailed in his confession. A few days after I left there I was horrified to hear of the murder of her Gentile husband —a Spaniard—and the evidence left no doubt in my mind that it was perpetrated by Hickman, assisted probably by one Bates, son of a Mormon bishop. It was reported that he had fled to the Southern part of Utah, and generally believed that he had taken refuge at Kanab, the new Mormon stronghold in the mountains bounding the Great Basin on the south, supposed also to be the hiding place of Burton (murderer of the Morrisites), Porter Rockwell, and other Danites, who, like Brigham Young, have "gone South for their health." But negotiations were in progress for his surrender, as detailed in his statement, and in August, 1871, he was brought to Camp Douglas. He is not confined, as, for obvious reasons, he would not dare return to any of the Mormon settlements, but has the freedom of the camp, with quarters and rations at the guard-room. From this place he sent me an invitation to visit him, and there I first met him face to face. I saw a man of heavy build, round head, and somewhat awkward, shuffling gait; five feet nine inches in height, with bright, but cold blue eyes, of extreme mobility, hair and beard dark auburn—the latter now tinged with gray—and a square, solid chin. His vitality is evidently great, and his muscles well developed. Our conversation need not be recorded, except to say that the man impressed me with his earnestness, and left me with a much better opinion of him than I had before. I then agreed to take charge of his manuscript, and, to use his own language, "Fix it up in shape, so people would understand it."

PREFACE.

My first intention was to re-write it entirely, speaking of Hickman in the third person; but one perusal satisfied me that it would be far better as he had written it. I have thought it best, also, to preserve his own phraseology nearly exactly, only inserting a word occasionally where absolutely necessary to prevent mistake. With very few exceptions, the narrative is precisely as written by Hickman, and, some faults of grammar and slang terms aside, I think every critic must admit that our sentimental and religious murderer has a singularly pleasing style. Neither have I thought it best to interrupt his narrative with explanations, but in the more important cases have added the corroborative evidence in an appendix. Late developments in Utah have poured a flood of light on many dark and bloody mysteries, and it is a great mistake to suppose that the recent criminal proceedings against Brigham Young and other leaders were founded upon the testimony of Hickman alone. He only supplied the clew which led to other evidence.

Notwithstanding the publications on the subject, many are still unacquainted with Mormon history. Hence I have given a brief outline thereof in the first chapter, which is submitted to the criticism of the reader.

J. H. BEADLE.

Salt Lake City, Dec. 10, 1870.

BRIGHAM YOUNG.

CHAPTER I.

INTRODUCTORY HISTORY.

BY THE EDITOR.

COMPARISON OF MORMONISM WITH OTHER SECTS—ITS INHERENT VICES—ITS ORIGIN AND SUBSEQUENT PHASES—THE "GOLDEN BIBLE" SPECULATION—THE "COMMUNITY" AT KIRTLAND—THE FANATICAL POWER IN MISSOURI, AND CONSEQUENT EXPULSION—NAUVOO—CRIME, POLITICS, AND WAR—FLIGHT WESTWARD—SETTLEMENT IN UTAH—HICKMAN COMES UPON THE SCENE.

MORMONISM, unfortunately for man's intellectual pride, is no new thing. From the earliest times history is full of the records of sects and races who imagined they alone had a right to the favor of God. For eighteen hundred years every generation has witnessed new revolts against the pure principle of "Peace on earth and good-will to men"—new sects of fanatics who would wrest the mild precepts of the Gospel, and deduce therefrom license for themselves, and a sanction for vengeance on their enemies. Most often—let the philosopher mark the strange and important fact—these perversions have touched the divinely established relations of the sexes: sometimes to grant one woman many husbands, sometimes to give one man many wives; at other times enforcing celibacy; and at still others setting up a complete sexual communism like the beasts of the field.

Inevitably such relations drew after them a mixed mass of social and political results: bloody and despotic governments, absolute power in the male head of the family or tribe, a religion of force untempered by mercy or love, jealousy, hatred, and unspeakable mutilation of young males. The Eunuch is the natural result of a polygamous society, and already several such cases have occurred in Utah.

The very name now blasphemously assumed by the Mormons—"Church of Jesus Christ of Latter-day-Saints"—was taken three centuries since by the bloody fanatics of Zwickau and Munster. And their doctrines were so similar to those held to-day in Utah as to excite the astonishment of the inquirer. Mormons in Germany in the time of Luther!

All these perversions of Scriptural marriage exist in some shape, in a few communities in America to-day— Shakers, Free-lovers, Communists, and Mormons. The last has developed the greatest strength, and been guilty of most cruelty and violation of law; and to a complete understanding of the personal narrative which follows, a brief account of the nature and history of the sect is necessary.

Mormonism is sanctified selfishness: a system which teaches practically that very little restraint need be put upon the baser passions; they can be religiously directed and piously cultivated; that the reward of obedience is not within the soul, a pure and hallowed delight, but temporal good and great power in the world to come, where a select few are to inherit all the good and all the others be their servants. To its adherents this gospel, not of humility and self-denial, but of pride and self-aggrandizement, promises substantially this: In a little while they will triumph over all their enemies, and every earthly power shall be put under them; the Saints shall possess the earth, and the unbelievers be trodden beneath their feet; all the farms and property in the country will ere long be theirs, the women and children be their wives and servants, and to all eternity they will glory over the Gentiles. Heaven itself would not be heaven to a good Mormon, unless he could have a few Gentiles to lord it over.

Of course such a sect can never be particularly dangerous, or any more than a local disturbance, to a free government; since it is the product of a previous mental slavery, and not of free institutions and free thought. But while it endures it is a grievous local tyranny, and on its members such doctrines must produce a terrible effect. In the very nature of the case, and under the mysterious moral law which governs the universe, such a belief cannot foster humility, long-suffering, charity to opponents, patient kindness, or universal love; its fruits are necessarily arrogance, spiritual pride, wild enthusiasm, and religious intolerance.

I invite the special attention of the reader who cares to inquire, to Mormon literature for the past forty years. In it you will find no deep contrition for sin, no earnest aspirations for humility, no heartfelt recognition of the brotherhood of man, no prayers "that all men everywhere might be free," no lively sympathy for philanthropic societies struggling against a sea of woes and troubles. On the contrary, all Mormon sermons and speeches can be compressed to just this: *"We* are the Lord's people, His chosen people, His peculiar people, to whom He has spoken by the mouth of His Prophet in these latter days; we know of a surety that our religion is right, and everybody else wrong, and the world hates us because we are right and they are wrong, and we have a perfect right to hate them because they hate us; the world has degenerated; there is no true religion, no real virtue outside of us; men are worse than in the days of Christ, and were worse then than in Abraham's day: the world is ripe and rotten ripe for the harvest of blood and death, and all hell is let loose to rage against the Saints!"

Can men who believe this sort of thing ever live in complete amity with their neighbors? That they *do* believe it I offer in evidence *all* their so-called theological works. (See P. P. Pratt's *Key to Theology;* Orson Pratt's *Works*—particularly *The Kingdom of God;* the *Journal of Discourses;* the *Voice of Warning;* and doctrinal sermons in old volumes of the *Millennial Star.*)

Nor is their social system other than organized selfishness. The Saint must marry many wives. Why? Because he will thus "build up his kingdom for eternity." But the numbers of the sexes being equal, even in Utah, he must build it *at somebody else's expense:* if he marries ten wives, nine other men must do without one apiece. He robs his brethren of any kingdom in order to build up his own. Hence the logical necessity of the doctrine, so carefully taught in the works of Pratt and Spencer, that *only the righteous are entitled to wives at all!* "It follows conclusively," says Pratt, "that from the wicked shall be taken away even the wife that he has, and she shall be given to the righteous man." Who the "righteous" are is, of course, already settled in their minds; the Gentiles, when things get properly fixed, are to have no wives. Can men who entertain such an idea of God's providences have much consideration for God's creatures? Will those who hold such low and imperfect notions of their neighbor's rights have regard for that neighbor's life, or liberty, or property, if he "stands in the way of the kingdom of God"? Can a man be much better than his ideal? Can the devotee rise above the standard of his *god?* Fortunately, most of the common Mormons have not quite entered into the spirit of, or "lived up to," their faith. They were recruited from the industrious, simple classes of northern Europe, and Mormonism has not entirely spoiled them. Nevertheless, I maintain that the ultimate effect of such a faith must be a selfish meanness.

Slavery and polygamy—"twin relics"—may well be put beside each other in a brief parallel. As of slavery thus: if a man will steal another man, steal his whole lifetime, his labor, his free-will to go and come—he shows thereby that he has taken one long step, if he is not some distance on the road, towards stealing any

other thing he can safely get away with. For what
greater good can he steal than a man's liberty and the
proceeds of his lifetime? Similarly of polygamy: if a
man will crucify the wife of his youth, and put her to
open shame, by introducing another woman into the
family, and calling her his wife, if he will make misery
for two helpless persons and pervert nature's current in
the breast of woman, whether for earthly lust or heav-
enly glory, he shows by that act that he will use another's misery for his own happiness, that he is a long
way on the road towards doing any other mean thing
which will give him an advantage over his fellow-man.
Hence a nation of slave-holders cannot long remain a
nation of freemen; a race of polygamists is sure to
become a race of self-seeking sensualists. Love, forgive-
ness, kindly charity, must wither in such an air. But
this argument, says one, touches the principle of freedom in belief. Granted: the hard fact still remains
that some religions are of such a nature that their reduc-
tion to practice would render their devotees utterly unfit
for amity or even neighborhood with civilized society.
The world has known scores of such religions; soon or
late they have one and all come into violent contact with
government or society, and yielded or been crushed. A
religion which makes it the chief hope of its devotee to
crush his opponents, not to convert or soften and unite
with them, can produce but one class of fruits: hatred,
malice, and all uncharitableness, strife and animosity
against all who dissent. Hence the Mormon's bitter
hatred of "apostates." Other churches pray for the

backslider; the Mormon curses them with hideous blasphemy. Said Heber Kimball: "I *do* pray for my enemies; I pray God Almighty to damn them." Said Brigham Young, in his sermon against the "Gladdenites" (*Journal of Discourses,* Vol. I., p. 82): "Now keep your tongues still, or sudden destruction will come upon you. Rather than apostates shall flourish here, I will unsheathe my bowie-knife, and conquer or die. * * * Such a man should be cut off just below the ears." And again, "I would take that bosom pin I used to wear at Nauvoo, and cut his d——d throat from ear to ear and say, 'Go to hell across lots.'" If such words were spoken in the pulpit and published *by the Church,* what may we not suspect to have been said and done in secret? Nevertheless, some apologists maintain that the Mormons, despite such a religion, would be first-rate citizens, "if let alone, and granted a State government." Can a bitter fountain send forth sweet water? can a people's whole inner life be bad, and their outer life good? If the Mormons are truly that peaceful, quiet, and industrious people we sometimes hear of, fitted for good citizens, *why* have they come into violent conflict with the people in all their seven places of settlement? For they have tried every different kind of people, from New York through Ohio, Illinois, and Missouri, to Salt Lake. Are *all* the people of *all* those places incurably vicious, mobbers and trespassers on religious right? This is your only possible conclusion, if you start with the hypothesis that the Mormon religion makes its devotees good citizens. The position is false; the facts are patent, and sound reason points to but one conclusion: the organization of the Mormon Church is such that it cannot exist under a republican government or in a civilized country without constant collision. This is a strong statement, but as a little monarchy could not exist in one country of an American State, as the Pope's temporality could not continue in the middle of Victor Emanuel's kingdom, so an ecclesiastical organization like that of the Mormon Church cannot peaceably continue in America. It is idle to talk of any compromise, such as Statehood by abandoning polygamy. The Church is a political entity claiming absolute temporal power within its jurisdiction; it must subjugate or be subjugated; it must rule the country it occupies or cease to exist. The conflict in some shape is inevitable. Mormonism is Mohammedanism Yankeeized. What Mahomet sought by his followers' swords, it seeks by subtle means, by perverting the machinery of free government.

The history of Mormonism is an exhibit of the foregoing principles reduced to practice; a series of attempts by the Church to erect local sovereignties, each defeated by government or people. It has presented no less than five distinct phases.

I. The first was that of the Golden Bible speculation. For the best evidence now shows that Smith and Rigdon scarcely hoped for anything more at first than to create a *furore* over the "Manuscript Found," and make money by the sale of the work, and that they were as much astonished as anyone else when they found the

Mormon Tabernacle, in which Brigham advised his followers to "Send the damn'd Apostates to hell across lots." See Appendix L.

matter making converts. But they were shrewd and knavish enough to use their advantage, and thus the speculation was the beginning of a new religion. The Pratts came into the organization a few months after; but Mormonism, as it stood for many years, as the basis now stands, was the joint work of Joe Smith, Sidney Rigdon, Orson Pratt, and Parley P. Pratt. It is not known that Brigham Young is the author of any distinct doctrine.

But, although converts multiplied, the authors were too near home to work successfully. The young Church emigrated to Ohio, almost in a body, and entered upon another stage.

II. The second phase of Mormonism was as a "Communistic Society," an experiment in religious co-operation, in Kirtland, Ohio. There the "Order of Enoch" was first revealed to Joe Smith, and at that period of Mormon history we first get a glimpse of the "Perfect Oneness" which afterwards played such a part in Illinois. The "revelation" for the first, stripped of all its verbiage, its "verily saith the Lord," and "my servant, Joseph Smith, Junior," simply means this: Each member is to deed his property to the Church or bishop, and hold it as steward, while all outside commerce is to be managed on a joint-stock principle. This has proved most difficult to introduce of all the Mormon schemes, though it has been revived several times since.

The "Perfect Oneness" consisted of an organization of the brethren into quorums of five, over each of which one was a sort of guardian; the property of the others was deeded to this one, so that in case of "vexatious lawsuits," as the Mormons style all suits brought against them, they could prove that it belonged to whichever one was necessary in order to defeat the execution. The Prophet had exercised a great deal of perverted ingenuity on these matters; but it requires no prophet to state the inevitable result. They could, of course, have no other effect than to cause all neighboring people to look upon the community with utter detestation. A mill was erected, a store opened, and a bank established upon the new principle. The brethren were credited at the store, or tithing receipts were accepted, or the goods were let out as pay to workmen on the temple. The result was, when Smith's notes fell due to Eastern dealers, he was unable to meet them; his creditors sued his endorsers, wealthy Mormons who had embarked in the joint-stock scheme; judgment was rendered; the Gentile obtained a judgment; the Mormons "beat them on the execution," and "persecution" followed as a matter of course. The bank enabled them to put off the evil day for a while. It was what was then—in the unsettled condition of banking laws in the Western States—denominated a "wild-cat" bank—that is, it had no charter from the State, and deposited no stocks as security, but its credit rested solely on the wealth of the projectors. Many Western men will remember the multiplicity of such institutions about that time (1830-40), and more than one "Hoosier" will think of the "Brandon Bank Paper," "John Watson Money," "Old Can*awl* Bank," and the "Kirtland Safety Society Bank," with a reflective sense of grief. The elders were sent out to put the notes of the bank in circulation, and worked so industriously at it that in a year they were worth but eight cents on the dollar. Mormons who had invested in these schemes apostatized and sued for their shares; they were thrust out of the community, and appealed to the Gentiles, and, in the words of Smith's Autobiography, "a hot persecution began." Several Mormons were badly treated in the neighborhood; Parley P. Pratt was "egged"; Joe Smith and Sidney Rigdon were tarred and feathered "for forgery, communism, and dishonorable dealing"—the mob said—and soon after fled from Kirtland to avoid arrest on civil process. The Kirtland branch of the Church soon followed, and the second stage of Mormonism came to an untimely end.

III. The third phase had already been inaugurated, in the form of a wild religious fanaticism in northwestern Missouri. Settlement had begun in Jackson County, Mo., soon after that at Kirtland, and by the spring of 1833 the Mormons there numbered 1,500. Joe Smith had visited the place two years before and delivered a voluminous revelation, which may be found in the *Doctrine and Covenants,* stating that the whole land was the property "of the Lord and His Saints. * * * The temple shall be upon the center spot lying westward of the town of Independence. * * * * Wherefore it is wisdom that my Saints shall obtain an inheritance in the land. * * * howbeit, the land shall not be obtained *but by purchase or by blood."* This was certainly an unfortunate beginning for people who wished to live at peace with their new neighbors. The old settlers laughed at these pretensions, and were threatened with damnation. But real earthly danger soon menaced them: in one year more, at their rate of increase, the Mormons would outnumber the citizens and get complete control of the county, and there was already ill feeling enough for the latter to conjecture too well what kind of justice they would receive.

The Mormons now became loud and arrogant: they solemnly announced the judgment of God, immediate and bloody, on all who opposed them; their Sabbaths were spent in "experience meetings," "speaking in unknown tongues," and prophecies of blood upon the unbelievers; they threatened an alliance with neighboring Indian tribes, notified Gentiles that it was useless for them to open farms or settle there, prophesied at one time a pestilence which would depopulate the adjacent country, and at another a war, and proclaimed generally that in a short time "Gentiles and unbelievers would have neither name nor place in all the borders of Zion."

Of course all these matters were greatly magnified, and a thousand rumors spread about the intentions of these "bloody fanatics." It was said they intended to prophesy a pestilence, and then poison all the wells of the State to bring it about; that they were in league with the Indians to rise and massacre the old settlers; that numerous Mormons had secretly got the places of ferry-men, with intention to cause the death by drowning—by apparent accident—of their principal enemies, and that they had arrangements for secret incendiaries to burn near places unfavorable to their religion. About this time, also, we find the first hints of polygamy in Mormon documents, and the first charges of that vice by the Gentiles. The papers published all these matters with inflammatory comments, to which the Mormon paper and speakers responded with threats of defiance.

The "old settlers of Jackson County" then issued a call for a meeting "to provide for means of defense," which assemblage issued a public manifesto, which I condense to the principal points: "We cannot," says the address, "trust to the civil law when dealing with a people who do not respect oaths or agreements with those not of their faith. * * * And when they shall have gained control of the county, let the public judge how we should obtain justice at the hands of men who do not hesitate to depose on oath that they have conversed with the Savior, had visions of angels, and performed all the miracles of healing the sick and raising the dead. * * * Of their pretense to divine power, their blasphemous utterances, and the contemptible gibberish with which they habitually profane the Sabbath, we have nothing to say; vengeance belongs to God alone. * * * * * But in protection of our common rights, in justice to ourselves and families, and in view of the bright prospects which, if not nipped in the bud, await this young and growing community, we do most solemnly declare—

"That hereafter no Mormons, either individually or

collectively, shall be permitted to settle in Jackson County.

"That those now here on a definite pledge of removal in the future, shall be granted reasonable time in which to dispose of their land and wind up their business. * * * * * * Should any of the Mormons refuse to accede to these conditions, they are referred to those of the brethren who have the gifts of divination and unknown tongues, to learn what fate awaits them."

This sarcastic conclusion was acted upon in serious earnest. The Mormons refused to leave, the citizens rose against them, a sort of civil war ensued, and the Mormons were driven across the Missouri into Clay County with some acts of extreme cruelty.

The Jacksonians have been much blamed for this action, and, indeed, they have but one excuse: either they or the Mormons *must* leave Jackson; they did not want to go, and so the Mormons had to. With this view the Mormons practically coincide: the perfection of their church system is incompatible with other civilized societies, and cannot exist in the same neighborhood with them. When they become tolerant and amicable, they simply cease to be Mormons. Individual Mormons in Utah at the present time who are social and intimate with Gentiles, *always* apostatize; Mormonism only becomes peaceful with the world in the degree that it ceases to be Mormonism.

From Clay the Saints spread into Caldwell and other counties, where they prospered greatly for a while. Then political troubles arose. They voted as a unit, and scattered their forces in different counties, so as to wield the greatest possible political power. An anti-Mormon convention unanimously resolved that, "though it cost blood to prevent it, the rule of these counties shall never be given to Joseph Smith." Every species of crime was alleged against them, much of which was shown to be true in the local evidence, collected and published by the order of the State.

The same thing was repeated on a larger scale, with more political complications, in the counties north of the Missouri, and in the autumn of 1838 the entire sect was driven from the State.

IV. The fourth stage of Mormonism was as a political independency in Hancock County, Illinois. Six years of local tyranny produced the same effects there, and in 1846 an angry people expelled them violently from Illinois. Most of the native adherents abandoned it, and Mormonism ceased for the most part to be an American Church.

V. The fifth phase we find in Utah: an essentially foreign community, governed by a few swindling Yankees, holding to just so much of original Mormonism as serves their purpose. Here our history ceases to be general, and becomes personal; with the expulsion from Nauvoo, Hickman comes upon the scene as a prominent actor, and I leave him to speak for himself.

CHAPTER II.

HICKMAN'S NARRATIVE.

BIRTH AND EARLY LIFE—FIRST DEED OF DARING—KILLING THE PANTHER—EDUCATION—MARRIAGE—JOINS THE MORMONS—ACQUAINTANCE WITH JOSEPH SMITH—THE TROUBLES AT NAUVOO—HICKMAN IN PRISON—INGENIOUS ESCAPE—FIRST ACT OF VIOLENCE UNDER THE RULE OF BRIGHAM YOUNG—KILLING THE COUNTERFEITER—SHOOTING THE INDIANS—FLIGHT OF HICKMAN—ADVENTURES ON THE PLAINS—ARRIVAL AT SALT LAKE.

I was born the 16th of April, 1815, in Warren County, Kentucky. My parents were early settlers of the State of Virginia, I being the sixth generation on this North American continent. I had, according to my grandfather's story, twenty-one blood relatives in the Revolutionary War, and not a Tory among them, which fact, the last time I saw him, twenty-eight years ago, he was boasting of. He gave me a long lecture, telling me he was old, and did not expect to see me again; that he knew nothing about my religion, neither did he care; but I must promise him that I would always be true to my country, telling me of the hardships the old revolutioners underwent, and the inherent right that I had to this independent Government, which made impressions on my mind and feelings that will ever remain with me.

When I was three years old my father moved from Kentucky to Missouri, and settled on the Missouri River, in the town then known as Old Franklin, which is now, with almost the entire bottom, washed into the river. It was opposite where Booneville now is, where the wild Indians were roaming, and committing depredations all over that country. Men were killed while plowing in their fields, and occasionally an entire family brutally butchered by those savages, the Sacs and Foxes. But peace being made two years afterwards, my father moved forty miles north, near where Huntsville now is. A settlement of some twelve or fifteen families composed the whole population of that region. There were only two families north of us, and none west, so you can imagine the wild country in which I spent my boyhood. There was plenty of buffalo in less than a day's ride; elk, bear, deer, turkeys, and bees, no end to them, and panthers screaming almost every night, which, together with the howling of wolves and screeching of owls, was most terrific to one so young. But it soon became a kind of second nature, and I would, when I heard those dreadful panther screams, or an unusual howling of wolves, look at father first, then at mother (yes, many was the time), to see if I could detect any look of fear in either of them. When I did not, I could compose myself and be at ease; but when I noticed them watching or listening I would keep a breathless silence: and many was the time I could her my heart beat, apparently to me as loud as a pheasant drumming on a log. But all went well for a year or so, when the Indians made an-

Brigham's Residence, where he is now held a prisoner, without bail. See Appendix.

other raid on an exploring party who came from the Missouri River to look at the country north of us, several of the party being killed. This was only about ten miles from our settlement, and then it was all the families got together, and all the men except three went after the Indians. They found six whites who had been burned at one place, and two were missing who were never heard of. The men were gone a week or so, but did not overtake the Indians. Scouting parties were kept out for a long time, till the Indians left, and the country commenced being populated. Many of the people became very industrious, making good farms, and raising grain and stock in abundance; while others would follow hunting, and seemed to care for little else.

My father built the first grist-mill in that country, and it was run almost constantly day and night for four or five years, no other mill being within forty miles of it. At the age of ten or eleven years we had the first school in the neighborhood, but my father and mother both having a fair education, had taught me and my two younger brothers at home; so that when I commenced school I could spell, read, and write tolerably well. About this time we got a legislative grant of a new county, and Randolph, the county seat, was located six miles from father's. Then commenced horse-racing and whisky-drinking, the backwoods roughs trying their manhood by fighting, many of whom would get most brutally beaten before they would yield to their antagonists, frequently getting a finger bit off, or an ear or nose, and sometimes an eye pulled out. At the first election in the country, my father was elected magistrate, which office he held seven years, and he who afterward became my father-in-law, George Burckhardt, was elected representative of that county to the Missouri Legislature, which office he filled fourteen years. We had a three months' school in the neighborhood every fall after it commenced. About the time I was twelve or thirteen years old, I performed my first feat of bravery. My father had several hundred head of hogs which roamed the woods, and needed no feed except when the ground was frozen; then they would gather in, and with them wild ones, having tremendous teeth sticking out of their mouths, and they would attack persons frequently. My father sent me to the mill to feed the hogs out of the toll corn in the mill, at the same time telling me to look out for the wild boars. I finished and started to the house, which was three or four hundred yards, and had got about half-way, when I looked behind me and saw a huge wild boar coming full tilt after me, not more than fifty steps behind. I started homeward for life, and an old hunting dog met me at the top of his speed, almost knocking me down as he passed. After making a few jumps, I stopped and turned to see the fight; I saw a fearful gash in the dog's shoulder, but he had the boar by the ear, and that moment fear turned into anger, and saying to myself, "I will kill you or die in the attempt," I picked up what we then called a hand-spike, which lay by the roadside, and made for the hog. But I had to back three or four times, as he would run at me with the dog holding to him. After awhile

I got a blow across his back, which brought his hind parts to the ground. I followed up my blows, the old dog holding to him, notwithstanding he had received three severe wounds, one on his neck, which I thought would be fatal from the flowing of the blood. But, faithful to his young master, whenever I would shout, "Hold him tight, Catch," he would go in while I struck the boar on the back and loins. I then took out my pocket-knife and cut his ham-strings, then cut a hole in his side, and literally gutted him, a handful at a time. I saw him dying, and for the first time, after speaking to the dog, he let him go.

I went home all bloody, went in and met father; he looked at me and asked what was the matter. I told him. He turned pale, then said I must be mistaken. He shouldered his gun and went with me. The first thing I showed him was the dog; poor fellow, he had stopped bleeding, and lay stretched in the door-yard. Father said he had never seen such teeth before. He gave me orders not to go out any more until the hogs had all gone for the woods again. This was much talked of. Many men said that no money could have hired them to do what I had done.

About two years after this, in the spring, we had a twenty-acre field ready to plant in corn. It being a big day's work for all hands, we were out as soon as it was light. But when first up we heard the blood-hounds making an awful noise, and understood that they had something up a tree, but supposed it was nothing but a coon, which were plentiful. The hounds often took a hunt without anyone with them. They would tree coons and keep up their barking and howling until morning, when some of us would go and see what they had, and thus get the game by cutting down the tree, or shooting the animal. But this morning there was an unusual amount of barking, as though there was something more than coons, and father said to me, "Bill, take the gun, and go and see what those dogs have treed." I started with a gun and knife, went about half a mile, and saw in a tree a large, full-grown panther, and the dogs under the tree. The hair stood straight upon my head; but I roused my courage, cocked my gun, and approached within fifty yards of the tree, when the savage-looking monster spied me. He leaped from the tree, and the dogs, six in number, four blood-hounds and two strong curs, caught him. I ran up, but there was such a turning and rolling that I feared to shoot, seeing no chance to do so without hitting some of the dogs. I drew my knife, as I saw him stretched by the dogs, and made a lunge for him; but he saw me, and made another effort, breaking loose from the cur that had him by the neck, and reached his paw for me, making a heavy stroke. He caught my pants just below the waist-band, and took out a strip about three inches wide, clear to the bottom. I turned and saw the dogs had covered him almost, but he was getting up, some having hold one place and some another. All his legs were held by the dogs but one. I made a sudden break, and stabbed him through the heart the first blow, jumped back, and shouted to the dogs. I saw him weaken, and soon he was dead. He was too heavy for me to carry; it was all I wanted to do to lift him. I went home and told the news, but was not believed until we went and packed the huge animal in. My pants I had tied up with hickory bark until I got home. The story about the strip torn out of them was too big to be believed, and they said it was not so—that I had torn them on a snag, or running through the brush; but when we went to get him the strip was in his claws, and stuck fast, and that was evidence beyond doubt that I had run a great risk, and I was strongly reprimanded for it. I loved sport, such as hunting and fishing, when I got the chance, and was full of mischief, such as tricks for fun-making, but I scarcely ever had a fight with a neighbor boy. I was strictly raised by a very quiet father and mother. I never saw my father drunk, nor heard him swear an oath; and can say more than most men, that I never knew my father and mother to quarrel. I have heard father say since I was grown that I was the best and worst boy he had raised: the best to work and do business, but doing more mischief than all the rest.

At the age of fifteen I was sent away from home to school. I was urged to go to the study of medicine, and did, but after a few months I gave it up, and went to school again. I was then urged to go to the study of the law, which I liked better; but became rather tired of that, and, seeing I had to be at books, I concluded I would go to school again. I was sent to another neighborhood, and boarded at George Burckhardt's, who was sending three of his family to the same school. I soon became charmed with one of his daughters. I thought she was the prettiest little black-eyed creature that ever lived. I was sixteen, and she was nearly three years older. This was my first love. She became attached to me, and when not studying we were engaged in social conversation. In four or five months we were engaged to be married when I got old enough. Our love increased, time went off slowly, and at the age of seventeen we concluded to get married. It was greatly opposed by my folks, in consequence of me being so young, and by my wife's father on the same account.

My father urged me to finish some study and then marry; but all this was no use. I was completely insaturated in love, and finally told father I would run away and get married, if he didn't give his consent. Finding our determination out, our parents both consented, and we were married, thirty-nine years ago last April. Our parents made no offer to assist us, waiting, as I understood afterwards, to see what I was going to do. After a few days I went to a neighborhood ten miles off, and hired to keep school six months, which I did, giving great satisfaction. I had a large school, some seventy-five scholars, and all learned well. My employers said it was worth more to them than all the schools they ever had before.

During this summer the Indians made a break on the North settlement, killed seven or eight men, and burned them. The news came, and volunteers were called for, in a great hurry. I was on hand and anxious to go, but my employers told me I must stay and teach their chil-

Young Hickman's first deed of daring. Killing the wild boar. Page 29.

dren. This was very grievous to me, it being the first chance I had to go to war. I reluctantly stayed. Some two hundred volunteers went, but found no Indians. The next winter a party of, I think, fifteen went on the sly, as they said, to beat Mr. Indian at his own game. They killed about a dozen, and all returned safe.

At the expiration of my school, my father gave me a tract of land, prairie and timber joined together, without any improvements, furnished me with the necessary tools, and told me to go to work. I built a house, fenced a farm, and continued to improve as long as I stayed in Missouri. I had three hundred and twenty acres of land, when I sold to go to Illinois, with good buildings on it.

Some eight or ten months after I was married, I joined the Methodist Church, which my wife belonged to when we were married. I lived a quiet and religious life, making theology my principal study. I investigated every religious belief I had ever heard of, and among the balance Mormonism, which I had supposed was trivial and trashy, but soon found I was mistaken. I continued to investigate it for two years. I lived on the road which the Mormons traveled from Kirtland, Ohio, to western Missouri, and had almost daily opportunities to talk with them. Being thoroughly convinced they were right, I joined them in the spring before they left Missouri. This was a great task for me. I had a good standing in society; the Mormons were very much disliked by the Missourians, and there was much sorrow expressed by friends and relatives for my joining them.

But I told them I was honest in my convictions, which was true. Nothing but salvation could have induced me to do so. The particulars of my conviction I could give, but do not deem it necessary to do so in this history; but suffice it to say there was no hypocrisy in me for so doing. My motives were pure, and my intentions good. Six months after the difficulties with the Missourians and Mormons took place in western Missouri, I lived something over a hundred miles east of where the Mormons were, and knew nothing of that difficulty only what I heard from both sides. My opinion was then, and is yet, that the Mormons were greatly wronged and abused. But doubtless, from their own admissions to me they had bad men among them, who committed some overt acts; but it was not a general thing, the most of them being quiet people. This to some extent could be accounted for. The most of the western wilds had at least two-thirds of their population of those illiterate, superstitious persons who had continued to keep on the frontier. This kind of people went *en masse,* carried elections, said what should be done, &c.

I had some trouble before I got away, which was the first, I might say, in my life, but it was with a gang of roughs who sought a victory over a Mormon. We had a nice little brickbat combat, in which two out of five got badly bruised. I answered for this before the magistrate, but the complainants failed to attend, having received word from me that the ball would open in a more serious way if they came there and swore to such things as they had to to obtain a warrant for me.

I sold my farm for a low figure, and left for Illinois. I saw much suffering and distress amongst those who were leaving Missouri: women and children barefooted and hungry; but these things were soon remedied. Our people were helped in Illinois, got work to do, and could get anything they needed for it. I gave away as long as I had a dollar, to those sufferers.

In April following I saw Joseph Smith for the first time, and had a long talk with him, and liked him well. I spent a year in Hancock County, and then went to Nauvoo and stayed another year; then moved back in the country, and stayed until the spring of 1844. Going to Nauvoo frequently, I heard Smith preach several times. I considered his preaching Bible doctrine. Heard him speak of the United States Government several times, which he always did in the highest terms. I heard him say once in a public audience that the Constitution of the United States was a part of his religion, and a good part, too. He said we were a cried-down people, and misrepresented, but should there come war in his day, he would show to the people who was true and loyal to their Government. Said he: "I would call on all the able-bodied men and go at their head, and the world should know what we could do."

Such assertions were often made by him. He said he was satisfied there would be war in which the United States would be engaged, but he did not expect to live to see it. "Now," said he, "brethren and friends, if any of you have anything against me, come and tell me, and I will make it right; do not be backward; come publicly or privately and see if I don't satisfy you or anyone that has anything against me." (What a difference between him and some who are now in his place.) In the spring of 1844 my wife and family went to Missouri to spend the summer with our relations, who had been anxious for us to move back ever since we left.

During this summer, difficulty arose in and about Nauvoo. Mobs raised, and the State authorities were called to settle it, Governor Ford being at their head. The Smiths were arrested, and placed in Carthage jail, eighteen miles from Nauvoo, with a flimsy guard over them. Governor Ford went to Nauvoo on some pretense or other, I suppose no person knows what, and while he was there, a blacked mob of eighty men drove the guard off and killed Joseph and Hyrum Smith. No exertions were ever made to arrest and bring to justice those mobocratic murderers.* I heard this while in Missouri, took my horse and went to Nauvoo, some one hundred and fifty miles; found everything as it had been told me, and the people in a sad-feeling state.

In the fall Brigham Young assumed authority to the leadership of the Church, which seemed in part to quiet the people; but with many it was no go. They would say: "He is no prophet; he was not called of God nor ordained by the prophet Joseph." I, being so thoroughly convinced of the truth of Mormonism, was willing to accept anything rather than say our system of things should fail. Things remained quiet until the next summer, when mobism commenced again. The next thing

*See Appendix—A.

was burning houses, barns, and grain, and haystacks of all Mormons living in the country around Nauvoo. The sheriff, not a Mormon, did all he could to prevent this, but it was of no use, the mob was too strong for him. He then called in a *posse* of Mormons to subdue those house-burners, and two of them were killed by the sheriff's order when pursuing them after burning a house. Grain-stacks were set on fire in the night, and the owners shot by the light when coming to see what caused it. This ended in the fall of 1845. Late in 1844 I went to what was called Green Plains, some twenty miles below Nauvoo, to Col. Williams', who, I was told, commanded the blacked mob who killed the Smiths, partly by request of Brigham Young, and partly to satisfy myself as to the cause of their death. I stayed with him one night. He was very jealous of me when I first went to his house, supposing me to be a Mormon; but I soon satisfied him I was from Missouri. I knew several of his relatives and friends who lived in the neighborhood I had just left, which soon dispersed all his suspicion, and a free conversation took place between us. He told me all about the Smiths being killed. I asked him what were the charges against them? He said they ruled the county, elected whom they pleased, and the old settlers had no chance; that it was the only way they could get rid of them. After getting through, he said: "Now, Mr. Hickman, we don't pretend to justify ourselves in what we have done; we frequently talk about it, but what else could we have done? There are some bad men amongst them who do some stealing, and it is almost impossible to catch them; but many of them are good men. I have them for neighbors, and have had them hired to work for me, and they were good neighbors and industrious." I also learned from him that they had no intention of mob-raising again, which was what Brigham Young wanted to find out. I went to Warsaw and around the country generally, and got the general say-so of all that class of men; returned to Nauvoo and gave general satisfaction to Brigham Young, this being my first business with him and my first acquaintance personally. I became more personally acquainted with him afterwards, and soon became satisfied he was no such a man as Smith, and really came to the conclusion it was a curse sent on us, that we were not worthy to have so good a man as Smith to preside over us; but I contented myself on the grounds that it was the best I could do, and by following his counsel the Lord would bless us with another like Smith.

In the fall and winter of 1846 there was much uneasiness amongst the people. They concluded to go West, and worked all winter making wagons, harness, and a general outfitting. The majority left, I think, in March, having organized previously in companies. I started with them in what was known as the Artillery Company. Colonel John Scott had that company in charge. We had four pieces of artillery, and some five hundred stands of small arms. Scott had four companies in his division, I being first captain. After a hard and lasting journey, we arrived at Council Bluffs, where United States officers came to our camp and made a call for five hundred volunteers, which were raised and joined the United States army, then fighting Mexicans. I was sick and not able to go, from the effects of measles. I stayed at Council Bluffs until I was able to travel, then went back to Nauvoo to bring on the family and assist others. When I reached Nauvoo I heard that a mob had taken Phineas Young and his son, and they could not be found; but were heard of, sometimes in one place and then in another. We raised a company and ransacked the country for some ten days before we got them. They had not been mistreated, only by threats and exposure, having been kept in the woods. Immediately after this, those ramparts of Illinois swore the Mormons should all leave forthwith. Nauvoo had at this time a majority of what was called new citizens, most of whom did not want the Mormons to leave until they could sell their property. Those had purchased property of the Mormons who had previously left. The mob commenced gathering southeast of the town, on what was known as Hunter's farm. There was a committee of twelve men then in the city, sent by the governor to investigate and see what was wrong. Satisfaction was given them on the part of the people of the city, and a party was sent to the governor. They did not return at the appointed time, and the balance went and did not return. The mob kept gathering, and the Mormons and New Citizens (Gentiles) gathered and resolved to withstand them. There were about two hundred in all that we could muster. Then skirmishing commenced on both sides. I should think that some six or seven hundred had gathered on the Hunter farm. We kept our guards out, and one day our picket was chased into the city near where our forces were. We enquired how many there were after them, and learned about eight. Captain William Cutler then made a selection of four men, all mounted on the best of horses, and went in pursuit. I was one of the party. We could not catch them, but chased them into camp, stopping out of gunshot distance. We stood up in our saddles and gave them as big a blackguarding as our tongues could utter: but no move was made for us. We were there some fifteen or twenty minutes between two sod fences—no show to cross, either—when we looked down the road and saw them getting on the fence behind us. We had to pass them or surrender. I began to think we had stayed a little too long. We started at full speed, and they mounted the fence as thick as blackbirds, I thought, crying, "Halt! halt! !" But no halt; we went through in a rain of bullets and no one hurt—one horse wounded. I had three cuts on my clothes.

The next day they moved around on what was known as Laws farm, where they would have a fair sweep at the city, and commenced cannonading. The scattering families who then lived in the east part of the town moved to the flat on the river. We had no cannon, but cut into a steamboat's shaft, plugged it up, fixed it up on wagon-wheels, hammered out balls of pig lead, which was plenty, and responded to the cannon-balls. This was the same size as their guns. They had three pieces, **and** we had two, which shot equally as strong **as theirs,**

Hickman in Prison at Nauvoo—Kills his Jailer and escapes. Page 45

but not so accurate. This cannonading was kept up for several days, while their party continued to increase, and ours to decrease. Men left when they pleased, and came when they pleased. We had blockaded some of the streets which we expected them to come in on. I belonged to a picket company, thirty of us, under Captain Anderson. They started for the city, and we were placed on the north, expecting them to come that way; but they swung to the south of our breast-works. Captain Anderson took his company just far enough in town to be under cover, and then marched us in front of not less than eight hundred men, who were keeping up a constant fire. But here let me say that while making this swing we passed one of our cannons where one man lay dead, with his head almost shot off. A New Citizen, a Methodist preacher, had the charge of it. He loaded behind a brick house, and would then roll it out and fire. He had just got it out when we reached his stand. The good old Christian prayed God that it might take the desired effect. I could not keep from laughing to hear such a prayer from such a man under such circumstances. Our company made breast-works of a brick house, log barn, and some large corn shocks, all close together, without being seen. When the enemy got within one hundred and fifty yards of us, we opened fire on them, which called them to a halt—but didn't the balls come thick! We thirty had about three hundred shots in repeating rifles, which we handled lively. Our captain was shot and fell dead at the commencement of the fight. At this time the other companies were playing on their right. About the time we had emptied all our shots and were ready to give way, the mob commenced a retreat, which was quite acceptable. We remained under cover, and reloaded as fast as possible. About that time we saw them coming again. They were halted as before and soon left, again going to their quarters. How many were killed I never learned. I had been anxious from a boy to be in a battle, but I assure you this fight took a great deal of starch out of me. My appetite for such fun has never been so craving since.

We saw our forces weakening, and knew eventually we should have to surrender; so we sent a flag of truce with committee to settle in some way the existing war. Terms were agreed upon, which was that the Mormons must forthwith leave; that they must all come in town the next day, unmolested, and have any and all persons delivered up to them they wanted, some dozen or so— among the lot was myself. This was the first time I began to be known. We thought we would cross the river that night and go westward; but the wind rose, and it was impossible. The others concluded to hide up another day, and then leave. I did not want to take chances in being found, so dressed myself in a number one suit of black broadcloth, fine boots, and kid gloves —a perfect disguise—and went to the ferry-boat; but just as I was leaving the shore I was recognized by one of their party. I was arrested, of course, and taken to prison to await the settling of other affairs, and then they would look into my case. I had sit feet of log-

chain put on my leg, with a fifteen-pound ball on the
end of it, and was locked in behind two doors. I stayed
a few days, and when the jailer came in one afternoon,
I knocked him down, took his bowie-knife and cut the
chain off my leg, took his pistols and left, and have not
been back since, which was about twenty-five years ago.
This was the only time I was ever in prison. I went
west on Grand River, in the southern part of Iowa. I
had lost almost all my property, so I went to work, raised
a good crop, made a horse-race or two, and by the next
fall was able to go on to Council Bluffs. Brigham
Young had been to Salt Lake with a pioneering party,
and returned to what was known then as winter quarters, now Florence, some eight miles from Council
Bluffs, across the river. I met him and party who had
come on our side of the river for the purpose of holding
the Fall Conference. I had a pair of beautiful ponies,
and Young wanted one of them for his son Joseph. I
gave it to him, keeping my running one, which had
made me several dollars before coming to that place.
I made a race with a Potowatamie trader, for three yoke
of oxen a side. It was opposed by my friends so strongly that I withdrew the stakes soon after. Brigham
Young then sent for me; I soon learned he wanted my
little race animal for his other son, Brigham, Jr. This
went against the grain, I knowing he had no use for
such an animal—that one worth one-fourth as much
would do him as well, and I told him so. "But," said
he, "if you keep her you will do wrong with her; you
will be racing, and I want her." I could not refuse,

believing, as I did, that he stood between God and His people, and could invoke blessings or cursings at pleasure.

The spring of 1848 rolled in. Young, Hyde, and others had some bitter enemies. One half-breed Indian from some of the tribes south, well-educated, had been to Nauvoo, joined the Church, gone home and had come to Council Bluffs to see Brigham Young. Brigham had made him very mad, and he was swearing vengeance. He said he was well acquainted with the tribes west, and would be out ahead of him, collect them together, and scalp Brigham Young before he reached Fort Laramie—that he would have a war-dance over his scalp in less than three months. Brigham Young's boys in winter quarters had got after him, but could not catch him, and he came on our side of the river. Brigham sent me word to look out for him. I found him, used him up, scalped him, and took his scalp to Brigham Young, saying: "Here is the scalp of the man who was going to have a war-dance over your scalp; you may now have one over his, if you wish." He took it and thanked me very much. He said in all probability I had saved his life, and that some day he would make me a great man in the kingdom. This was my first act of violence under the rule of Brigham Young. Soon after this, I was called upon to go for a notorious horse-thief, who had sworn to take the life of Orson Hyde. I socked him away, and made my report, which was very satisfactory. Hyde was well pleased, and said he knew I had saved his life.

In the spring of '48, Brigham's company started for Salt Lake, with their families. I, in company with a number of others, crossed the Missouri River and went thirty miles to Elkhorn River, to bid Brigham and party a good-bye. Brigham told me he wanted me to stop that year with Orson Hyde, as there were those around who might kill him. He wanted me to look out for him, and see that nobody hurt him. This was very satisfactory to Hyde. In about a month, Amasa Lyman, one of the Twelve, followed Brigham Young with another large company for Salt Lake. I had in the winter just previous to leaving Nauvoo taken me a second wife, whose father was going with this company, and she wanted to go with them. I sent her along, and when I reached Salt Lake next year was not surprised to find she had helped herself to a youngster a few days old. Believing her virtue to be easy long before this let me off. I never had any children by her. When bidding Brigham Young good-bye, in the spring of '48, he said to Orson Hyde: "If Brother William wants to take him another wife, you attend to the marriage ceremonies."

In the fall of '48, Orson Hyde got after a gang of counterfeiters, and put me on the track to ferret it out, if possible. Some of them were Mormons, some Gentiles, and some apostate Mormons, eight or ten altogether. They were making dollars and half-dollars; had dies and a screw-press, and were making what was called a good article of bogus money. About this time, Orson Hyde started a paper called the *Frontier Guardian,* and was giving these fellows a tremendous blowing up. They threatened his life, some of them being of the desperate kind. They also threatened to burn his printing office. Here was another job for me—to watch the printing office. I would go into it after dark, at the back door, well armed. A party came one very dark night, and burst the front door open; I fired two shots at random, but hit no one. This caused an abandonment of that project, but they were more enraged at him than ever. I threw myself in their company, and heard their threats, upon which I told them if they hurt a hair of his head, I would kill the last counterfeiter in the country, and to pitch in as soon as they liked, and I would turn loose upon the first one I heard make a threat. This caused them to be quiet, and soon they began to be discountenanced by the people. I found a portion of their press, which was destroyed. This broke them up, and gave my friend, Orson Hyde, much relief of mind, he not having the nerve that a military general should have. He said I had again saved his life, which thing he often spoke of, and sometimes would preach it to his congregation. But when Brigham Young says the word, all the dogs howl, and this Hyde has not ventured to speak to me for a long time.

During the summer of '48 some Omaha Indians were crossing the river, and driving off the stock belonging to the people. They took the last animal belonging to several. We would go in search, but would find where they had crossed the river, which always ended pursuit. A boy in the town came in and told me he had seen two

Indians in the brush about a mile off. I took my pistol and knife, telling the boy not to tell anyone else, and went in search, crawling through the brush with all the quietness of a cat after a mouse. My object in telling the boy not to tell anyone else was to keep the people from making a rush, as they would frighten the Indians, and they would get away as before. After watching about an hour, I saw three Indians with ropes and bridles, and armed with bows and arrows. I took deliberate aim, having two in range; one fell, and one ran towards me, the third ran the other way. The one that ran towards me fell about three rods off. The ball had cut the back of his head, and made him crazy; but I was to him as he rose, and shot him dead. I took their bows, arrows, ropes, and bridles, and put them in a pile, went to town, told a few of my friends, who were well pleased, but thought we had best say nothing about it, as there might be some exceptions taken to it by United States agents. The Indians were left until night, and then buried. I worked hard that summer, building houses in the town known then as Kanesville.

The next winter a Government contractor took about one thousand head of oxen forty miles north of us to winter on the rush bottoms of the Missouri River. Early in the spring this agent said a gang of thieves were stealing his cattle, and scattering them over the country, altering the U. S. brand on them, and killing some. He came to Kanesville, got a writ, deputized a man and *posse* of four to go and arrest them. They returned

whipped out, and no prisoners, upon which this agent
went to see Orson Hyde, and asked him if he had not
men who could and would arrest this party. I was sent
for, and introduced to this agent, who I found to be a
clever man and a gentleman. He filled my pocket with
money, saying: "Go it, my man, and fetch the rascals,
and I will see that you get many a dollar for it."

Next morning I started with my one man, a good
one, too. We were well armed. I got within a few
miles of their place, stayed that night, and next morning we were upon them early. There were four guns
drawn on us with the word to stand. I looked in their
eyes, and did not see a shoot in them. It was all bluff.
We drew up our guns and ordered an immediate surrender, or we would turn loose on them. They came to
time, and we arrested four. We went to another place,
and got two. One of them had strong indications of
shooting. I tied his hands behind him, summoned another man, and returned with the six prisoners amid
shouts. I assisted this man in getting his scattered and
stolen stock, for which he paid me roundly, which enabled me to have a good and sufficient outfit for Salt
Lake, where I was intending to go that spring. I commenced getting ready; gathered up, and crossed the
river in company with a few other families, to await the
starting of the first Mormon train, not forgetting the
liberty given to me by Brigham Young to get another
wife, which I did. She was a good, industrious woman,
kind-hearted and agreeable: her mother was dead, and
her father and only brother were in the Mexican War.

I brought her across the plains, and found her father and brother in Salt Lake, glad to meet her.

While laying on the west side of the river, Orson Hyde sent for me. I got to Kanesville in the afternoon, and found a horse saddled, and four men waiting for me with horses also. I learned that twelve or fifteen Indians were then in the brush some five miles off. Orson Hyde gave us our instructions, and told us to be sure they did not all get back across the river. We struck out, following our guide, learned where the Indians were, and made a descent on them. The Indian I went for turned two arrows loose at me. I shot him down, and made a dash for another, shot him down, whirled to see what the other boys were doing, and found them whipping two Indians. They had not fired a shot. I concluded I had done my part, and stopped. Our report was all satisfactory. I started before day to our camp across the Missouri River, and that day got word from Orson Hyde to roll out with some California train at once, for h—ll was popping about those Indians that were killed on a United States reserve. We rolled out that evening twelve miles, and fell in with Colonel Cornwall's train, bound for the California gold-mines, from Illinois, who willingly accepted our company. I found him a gentleman; we had a good time on the plains, and a big dance with the Mormon girls when we reached Salt Lake. He was an old Indian-fighter; had commanded an expedition against the well-known warrior Black Hawk, in '32, and had slain many of them. The Colonel went on to California that fall. We got into

"I turned my old yauger loose, and he fell." Page 54.

Salt Lake August 20, '49. The Colonel has made several trips across the plains since, taking stock to California. He always called and spent a few days with me, and we never failed to have a good time.

We found plenty of game on the plains, such as buffalo and antelope. I was appointed one of the hunters for the company, which thing I enjoyed very much. I got laughed at one day for giving a jack-rabbit a chase, thinking it was a young antelope, it having started out from a band of them. It was the first one I had ever seen, and I thought it very strange that the young ones could outrun the grown ones.

Some few days after this, another hunter and myself left the train for a hunt, and were to meet it at night. We traveled ten or fifteen miles before we found any buffalo. We killed one, a fine fat cow, took on our horses about one hundred pounds each, and started for camp. We had not traveled more than three miles when we saw some forty or fifty Indians, to all appearances trying to get in ahead of us. We guessed their intention, cut our meat loose, and lit out for camp, at least fifteen miles off. We were far back in the sand-hills, a dreary-looking place. The Indians all held up but six, who put their ponies down to their best. We outran them for awhile, and then held our own for awhile, when my friend's horse, although a good one, was failing. I had a nail-driver, very swift, and no end to his bottom. I fell back as though my horse had failed. Five of the six halted their gait, and one came at full speed for me. I waited until the Indian was within two hundred yards of me, ran my horse around a mound and dismounted. I was not more than ready for him when he came in sight, not more than fifty steps off: I turned my old yauger loose, and he fell, holding his horse by the bridle. I mounted, rode out and saw the other Indians were in a short distance. I wanted the pony (he was pretty, and speckled as a bird), but was in too much of a hurry to get him. I started for my comrade, who was by this time a mile ahead. My horse carried me off at almost lightning speed. I kept a good lookout behind, but they came no farther than where I shot the Indian. This was a caution for us not to be caught so far from home, which caution we accepted of for the balance of the trip.

CHAPTER III.

FROM 1850 TO 1854.

FIRST YEAR IN UTAH—FIRST INDIAN WAR—LIEUT. J. W. GUNNISON—A SERIOUS DEFEAT—BETTER COUNSELS—A VICTORY—A BRAVE MILITIA OFFICER(?)—A BATTLE ON THE ICE—MASSACRE OF INDIANS—TAKING THE HEAD OF BIG ELK—HICKMAN GOES TO CALIFORNIA—CHOSEN CAPTAIN OF THE TRAIN—INDIAN MASSACRE AND MORE FIGHTING—A MURDER AND LYNCH LAW EXECUTION—TROUBLE IN UTAH AND RETURN OF HICKMAN—MURDER OF IKE HATCH—KILLING THE HORSE-THIEF—KILLING OF IKE VAUGHN—FIGHT BETWEEN THE MORMONS AND GREEN RIVER FERRYMEN—HICKMAN KILLS ANOTHER HORSE-THIEF—CRUELTY OF ORSON HYDE—DASTARDLY MURDER OF HARTLEY—COMMENTS.

After arriving in Salt Lake, I stopped a few days with one of my friends, then located the place ten miles south of the city, where I lived until five years ago. I went to work, and worked hard until in the winter.

At this time there was only two settlements in the valley south; the first was on American Fork, a stream some two or three rods wide, emptying into Utah Lake. The next was a settlement on Provo River, fifteen miles further south, some three miles from Utah Lake. This river was claimed by a strong band of Indians. These Utah Indians went by different names, such as Timpa-Utes, Pi-Utes, Yampa-Utes and Gosh-Utes, each having its Chief, fishing and hunting grounds, &c., which they claimed as their own; but in reality they were all the same tribe, spoke the same language, and would hunt and fish on each other's lands, as a general thing, unmolested. Sometimes these different bands would have difficulty; but in war with the whites they were all united.

This Provo band was considered very brave, having held that river for a long time. The Mormons got permission of them to settle there, and made them presents, and they were glad to have them come and raise grain. They petted and humored the Indians too much, and this winter they began to do as they pleased. They first commenced stealing their horses and cattle, and seeing they were not chastised for it, would take cattle or anything they wanted, and deliberately drive it off at any time, saying to the people, "You are all petticoats, and won't fight." This continued until in February, when they commenced shooting at the people if they tried to hinder them from taking anything they wanted. The people called for help from Salt Lake, and one hundred and fifty men were soon raised under charge of George Grant, to go and give them a clearing out. Among this company was Capt. W. H. Kimball, Adjutant Gen. Ferguson and the lamented Captain Gunnison, who was wintering in Salt Lake, with a Government party of topographical engineers under Colonel Stansbury. This military clever gentleman volunteered his services, and went with us. So did the Surgeon of that United States party, and a few others. The Captain was never behind, always showing skill and bravery. I became very much attached to him, and he was well liked by all as far as I knew. About 9 p. m. we got to the settlement at Provo, which was two or three miles west of where the city of Provo now is. I was sent ahead in charge of the advance guard.

All was quiet, and we got through their half fortified place without the Indians knowing of us, and made the necessary arrangements for quarters, forage and supper. I was sent for, and found a council of war was called, the object of which was to fix the *modus operandi* of an attack on the Indians the next morning, which were about three miles above us on the river, in thick brush and heavy cottonwood timber. Officers were appointed, and companies formed, all satisfactory, and then a display of talent from the new and highminded officers ensued.

The canteen passed around frequently, which inspired their minds, and made assurance of an early victory next morning. I was silent till Colonel Grant turned to me and said, "Well, Captain Bill, what have you got to say? I have not heard a word from you."

I told him I did not like any of their plans. I reasoned on the Indian mode of fighting, that they would resort to all sorts of stratagem and advantage, and in that light we should look at them, and against such movements lay our plans, which I had not heard proposed by any of his staff. I made a few more suggestions and stopped. The canteen passed again, and when it came my turn the Colonel said: "Bill, take a good one; you must be down at the heel." I drank a success for the morrow, after which the Colonel arose, gave orders that the cannon which we had taken with us, should be placed above on the south side of the river, that two small companies should be placed on the north side above and one below, and I should make a selection of twenty horsemen, with good horses, sabres and pistols; that those companies north, east and west, should charge on the camp (now this camp was supposed to contain one hundred warriors), and drive them out into fair ground, where I could, with my company, charge upon and chop them up.

I went to my quarters, studying whether it was the want of brains or too much canteen that had caused such plans. But, thought I to myself, if it suits you I am satisfied.

All set and off in the morning as per order. One of my men asked me as we were going to the field of battle, what I thought of their running the Indians out of the brush for us to kill. I told him I would agree to eat all the Indians we got a chance to kill that day. All reached their posts about nine o'clock. The sound of musketry was heard, and the roar of cannon, which was kept up all day. Occasionally we would see them packing off a dead or wounded man, but no Indians for us. The sun was about an hour and a half high, when I made a rush with my company of cavalry within a hundred yards of the Indian camp without orders, fired into them, wheeled and left for our place. Several balls whistled amongst us, but nobody was hurt.

Soon after this the bugle sounded a retreat, and the Indians set up such a yell of victory that one would think ten thousand devils had been turned loose. We went back to our quarters. Officers and men looked sad. Some of our men were killed, and some wounded. Supper being over, I was sent for again. I went in and looked around, but did not see a big feeling man amongst them. I felt rather tickled to see the contrast between that and the night before.

After talking over all that had transpired that day, I was the first one asked to say what should be done the next day. I told them that my plan of strategy and surprise would not work now, as the Indians knew we meant fight in earnest; that I saw no other way than to select the best Captains, and let them pick their companies, and take the brush, crawl up within gun shot, and play upon them, while the Colonel would be where he could see what was going on, and at any time in the afternoon that he thought fit, sound a charge on which a general rush was to be made to wind up the fight.

My plan was adopted without any opposition, and I was chosen for one of those brush Captains, and placed on the north, where the hottest fire had come from the day before. I got my men within eighty yards of their camp without being seen, and poured a volley of shots in amongst them, which made a great scattering and hiding. We got under cover of brush and banks, and whenever an Indian showed himself we would turn loose on

"I took the head, gun, bow and arrows, mounted my horse—took a pretty squaw behind me, and a sick papoose in front, and was off for my quarters." Page 68.

him. In this position we lay all day, in snow fifteen inches deep, but I never heard a man complain of being cold. The companies played upon them above and below. Capt. Kimball from in front, or rather from the south, made a rush to take a log house within gun shot of them, in which he had his horse shot dead under him. Kimball was both brave and venturesome.

Captain Conover, who had charge of the Company above me in the afternoon, laughingly asked me if my men were all there; I told him I thought so. He said I must be mistaken, and asked me if I had had any killed. I told him no; upon which he said: "One of your men is dead, the one that wore that tall hat." I looked around, and that one was gone. The Captain laughed again, saying: "He is dead. When I saw you bringing your men into position, I saw him stop about one hundred yards behind in a bunch of brush. The Indians saw him, and commenced shooting at him, when he left and ran close to me. I called to him to stop, but could not get him to halt, and saw him jump through the fork of a tree twelve feet high, and know he broke his neck before he stopped." Poor fellow; he luckily escaped, and was as brave a man as I had at the supper table.

This brave soldier is now one of the Colonels of the Utah militia, and expects to whip the United States when Brigham gives the word. Such men should be greatly feared, lest they get scared, and sure enough break their necks.

There was no charge sounded, but we knew we had done good execution that day. The Indians made a lamentable yell until the bugle sounded a retreat, then all was still. No shouts of victory or Indian yells were heard that evening. All went to quarters. Two days of fighting, and that breakfast spell of Indians not wiped out yet.

The next day was Sunday, and fighting was suspended. In the afternoon the Colonel took some fifty men, me with them, to ride around the Indian camp, and see how things looked. After some time I was satisfied there were no Indians there. I told the Colonel so, and urged him to make a charge on the camp, as there was plenty of us to use them up anyhow. He was not in favor of it. I fell behind, and when a good opportunity offered, made a dash through their camp; saw some children and some wounded; rode around quickly and out again, and called to the Colonel. He said they might be in ambush. Then James Hirons, as brave a man as I ever was with, came to me, and we dashed in again, and around, and then called to the company, who rushed in and found the Indians were gone.

The dead and wounded lay thick, only half-a-dozen sick children were left. Everything was burned, and we took with us the children, who were well taken care of. The next day we found the remainder had gone to the mountains, the snow being very deep there. We placed a guard at the mouth of the cañon, and went in search of other portions of the tribe in the south end of the valley. I was sent with a party of six to spy out the situation of the Indians on Spanish Fork, twelve miles south. We found the Indians encamped in the brush on the creek, and fifty or sixty head of horses feeding on fair ground close by. On our arrival in sight some of the Indians rushed out and drove their horses into the brush. On our return conversation was about the number of Indians we had seen. Some said thirty, some forty, and some sixty. I was riding with Captain Carus, a fine, clever old Dutchman. "ell," said he, "Villiam, how many do you say we saw." I told him twelve, for I had counted them; I mention this to show you how things multiply to persons when fear and excitement have possession of the inexperienced, such as these.

On the next day we marched for them, but on search, found a trail where they had left for the Utah Lake, some twelve or fifteen miles west. While searching I accidently spied an Indian in the brush, in all probability left as a rear guard. I rushed towards him; he shot two or three arrows at me, and wheeled to run. I shot at him, which made him bound through the brush, tearing off his quiver of arrows, but did not hit him.

Here I must stop and tell a story of my outfitting before leaving Salt Lake. One of the old fathers, sixty-five or seventy years of age, came and brought me his old-fashioned broad sword, asking me if I would accept it on this trip. I told him I would, and thank him, too; upon which the old man said: "May God bless and preserve you, and may I have the pleasure of cleaning it on your return." The Indian was scared by my pursuit, and going through the brush had about one hundred yards of a clear place to pass. I crowded my horse at his full strength through the brush, just keeping in sight of the Indian; but I thought of the request of the old man to clean his sword on my return, so I drew it, and before he got through the open space overtook him and made a heavy back-handed cut on his head. He fell, and I jumped off my horse and ran the sword through him, putting it up without wiping:

We then struck on the Indian trail, found them at dark encamped on the lake near the head. General Daniel H. Wells had just come to us on the Indian trail. He was Commander-in-Chief. He stationed guards around the Indian camp in order to prevent their escape during the night. This was a bitter cold night on the Lake shore—snow on the ground, and the wind blowing a gale. We had had no dinner, had no supper, no blankets, and nothing but sage-brush to make fires, and even that was scarce and small. The body of the men camped or rather stopped below, and took turns pulling this brush, which kept them from freezing.

I was placed above on the Lake shore with Lot Smith and John Little, Jr., who would take turns going to the fire, leaving one with me all the time. My orders were to stay until relieved. I walked my post and kept from freezing with much ado.

As soon as it got light I got orders at the sound of the bugle to charge their camp, and strange to say, I was alone when the charge was sounded. I ran up on the beach in order to give me a fair view of what was or would be going on. Firing commenced, and I saw an Indian coming towards me unnoticed by the company. I got behind a bush and waited until he was within eight feet of me, when I shot him dead, ran for the battle, and saw an Indian start on the ice. I ran him some three or four hundred yards, got within fifty steps of him and downed him, returned, and the battle was ended. Fourteen Indians lay almost in a pile. Some twenty odd were killed in all. General Wells started a party of fourteen of our men up the Lake bench to see if there was any more Indians near by. We had not gone more than two miles when we saw five Indians coming down the Lake shore on horseback, on the edge of the ice, which was about two feet thick, with a little snow on it. They turned back, and we after them. Here was a nice chase, but as usual, only three or four of us had horses fast enough to catch the Indians. I shot the first, Lot Smith the next, and I the next, who came near falling off his horse, but recovered. The savages were shooting back at us with rifles and arrows whenever we got close to them.

Lot was a brave man; whenever he emptied his gun he would get another and pitch in again. These guns were willingly handed him by those cautious fellows behind, and he emptied some half-dozen of them. I had a slide rifle; six shots in a slide, and three slides, making eighteen shots on hand. Lot shot at an Indian whose horse had fell on the ice and broke his gun, but he kept trying to shoot. We halted and gave him six or eight shots before he fell. One Indian alone was on his horse wounded, and I saw Lieut. R. T. Burton make a dash for him. He had a good horse, and I thought it no use to go any further, as Burton would be sure to get him. I watched him and saw him shoot off his pistols at the Indian when two or three hundred yards from him, and turn back. I mounted my horse, a good one, too, and crowded him for the Indian, who by this time was a mile ahead. He left the Lake and started across the bench for the mountains. I dismounted, took good aim at him, and fired; he fell, then rose and climbed over some rocks. I shot at him again, when he left his horse, went up the mountain about a hundred yards and fell dead.

I went to camp, and we had provisions sent to us, which were very acceptable, as we had had nothing to eat since breakfast the day before. We scouted the country a few days and went to Provo to go up the cañon and wind up the war. Two companies were sent up the canon, one under Captain Lameraux, and one under Captain Little. I was sent ahead as a spy with Mr. Hirons, of whom I have already spoken. We proceeded up the cañon some two or three miles, occasionally going up the side of the mountain so we could get a fair view of things ahead. We did not see anything for some time, when all at once we looked below and saw the Indians in a ravine not a hundred yards off. We had reached this place under cover, saw the Indian spies looking down the cañon, and knew from all appearances we had not been seen. "What shall we do?" said Hirons. I answered, "We will give them a shot apiece, and if they don't run, we will." "Pick your man so we won't both shoot at the same Indian," said he. We lay snug behind the rocks; the word was given by him, and we both fired, fetching our men. The Indians broke, and we fired again, but I do not think we hit any, as they were running. We threw ourselves in sight, and waived our handkerchiefs for the companies to come on. As far as we could see the Indians were running up the cañon.

We went down to see the Indians we had shot. Hirons told me I had killed the chief, Big Elk. I took off his head, for I had heard the old mountaineer, Jim Bridger, say he would give a hundred dollars for it. I tied it in his blanket and laid it on a flat rock; hid his gun and bow and arrows, forty-two number one good arrows, and awaited the arrival of the company. The reason I hid the above named articles was because I had tried to get some arrows or some relic to take home with me, from several of those *cautious* fellows who were great warriors, but not one could I get; they had all been taken by them to take home to show what victories they had achieved.

The companies soon came up, when we attacked and killed nearly all the Indians. We took about fifty women and children prisoners. When I came to where I had killed the chief, I had to laugh. Those rear fellows who had been in the habit of picking up everything, had untied the blanket that was around the chief's head, but on seeing what it contained left it untied with the head sitting in the middle of it, entirely untouched. I took the head, gun, bow and arrows, mounted my horse, took a pretty spuaw behind me and a sick *pappoose* in front, and was off for our quarters.

This wound up the Indian war of '49, so called, although it was in the spring of '50. We took the prisoners to the city, and distributed them among the people. The warriors were all killed but seven or eight, and the

"I hit him over the head, killing him instantly."—Page 75.

next spring all the prisoners that wanted to went to adjoining tribes.

All was peace and no Indian troubles for three years after this. I went to work on my farm, fencing and building, but had poor luck. Did not get the water out of the river so as to irrigate it in time. The California immigration began to come in. I had that spring purchased a few Indian ponies, and had them fat, just what the emigrants wanted. I spent the summer trading and herding stock. I herded the stock belonging to the Church and Brigham Young. I delivered them all to Brigham in the fall, having lost none, and charged him nothing. The bill should have been over one hundred dollars, but I made a good summer's trade and built more houses. In the fall I got my leg broke by a horse falling on it, and was lame for eight or ten months.

In the winter, Brigham Young saw me with a fine bay horse I had traded for that summer, and wanted him. I gave the horse to him.

I got the gold fever, and went to California in the fall of '51. Left Salt Lake in August, and went to Bear River north, on the California Road, where there were some emigrants organizing, and awaiting to get a good company, as the Indians had been very bad that year, killing sometimes an entire train. A few Mormon boys went, five I think. This was the last train that went through that year. It was composed of people from Missouri and Illinois, and Mormons, with two South Carolinians, making in all 42 men, six of them having their families along. Some had horses, some mules, and some ox teams, with a few head of loose cattle, and a dozen loose horses, but not one good riding horse. We all got together to organize for a start. When the meeting was called I was astonished to hear myself nominated for captain, as I was not acquainted with ten men in the company. I got up and objected, but this was of no use; they said that they had heard of me, those who did not know me, and had made up their minds to have me for their Captain; that we had to go through a country full of bad Indians, and they knew from what they had heard that I knew more about them than any other person in the company, and I had to accept.

I found I had a first rate set of fellows, several of whom had served in the Mexican war, and served in several battles, and one of Kit Carson's old Indian fighters, some old farmers from the States with their families, and, taken all together, a company that would be an honor to any man. The twentieth of August we started. The next company ahead of us had been gone two weeks, had horse and mule teams, and sixty-four men in the company.

All moved off nicely, until we got about four hundred miles on our road, and were traveling down the Humboldt River. There we began to see where wagons had been burned, and also skeletons of men, women and children, their long and beautiful hair hanging on the brush; and sometimes a head with as beautiful locks of hair as I ever saw, and sometimes those of little children, with two or three inches of flaky hair, either lying by or near them, the wolves having eaten the flesh off their bones. But all the bodies of the men, women and children that were found had a portion of the skin taken off the tops of their heads. They had all been scalped, and the savages, in all probability, as we talked of it, were then in the mountains having war-dances with the whoops and yells of demons, over these scalps of honesty and innocence.

Some of the boys began to get terribly riled up, and wanted to stop and hunt the Indians. Our train traveled snugly together and camped on clear ground, tying our horses at night, and corraling our cattle, always keeping out a strong guard. About this time we met the train coming back that had started ahead of us, having fought the Indians several days, lost nearly half of their stock, and twelve or thirteen of their men. They advised us to turn back, assuring us there was no show to get through. We thought differently, and some of the boys laughed at them. Finding out we were determined they turned to go with us, but told us they had traveled and fought Indians all day only three days before. As we journeyed, with the new company in our rear, all at once there was a dash, a hoot and a yell from the brush about three hundred yards off. The train was halted; twenty-five of my men in less than a minute had their guns, about half of us mounted our horses, the balance on foot, and instead of waiting for them to circle and fight we went for them, telling at the same time the other company to remain still and take care of the teams.

The Indians had made no arrangements for a retreat,

but ran into the willow brush on the river, which was fordable anywhere, and after them we went. They took a fright like a gang of wild antelopes, and ran in all directions. We popped them right and left until all were out of sight. I flew around on my horse to see the boys, fearing I had lost some of them, but all were safe. Two were slightly wounded. All swore they would scalp the Indians, and have a war-dance over their scalps. I told them to do as they pleased. They got thirty-two scalps off of the Indians killed on the ground, and what gave my men increased anger, one of the Indians was found with the scalps of two women, cured and dried, and another had the scalp of a child, I should think not more than three or four years of age. I need not tell you—you may guess the feeling that existed.

We all had a great war-dance that night. Our friends from the company behind us came over and declared positively they had never seen such men before; said it was a wonder we were not all killed, and declared they saw one hundred and fifty Indians. The boys seemed easy for a day or two, but on finding another quantity of bodies became anxious for another fight.

We traveled quietly for probably one hundred miles, when four Indians were seen crawling through the sage brush towards our stock; we went for and got them; killed and scalped them. We were now getting toward the sink of the Humboldt, and began to see a great many fresh Indian tracks. The next day they seemed to be gathering in from all directions to about the place we intended camping. The sun was about two hours high when we discovered them on the bench, and in the willow brush on the opposite side of the river. I kept the train moving until we got into a low place out of their sight, when we halted, and the men got their guns and mounted in short notice. We had twenty-six men ready. I wanted the company behind to take hand in the fight, but the boys would not agree to it.

We got within gun shot of the Indians before they saw us. The boys made a rush on them, shooting, hooting, and yelling in such a manner that they all took fright before firing a gun or shooting an arrow. The boys dashed into the brush, keeping up a constant firing, and the Indians rose around us as thick almost as a gang of sheep. I never saw the like. They took down the river into large and thick brush. I saw up the hill, about a mile off, one of my men after an Indian. He shot at him, wheeled his horse, and started back. I had just emptied one slide of my gun, six loads, and had no other slide with me. One of my men had a good rifle, which I took and started at full speed over the sage brush, met the man and asked him what was the matter. He said he had shot off his gun and both pistols, and had no more ammunition with him. In about two miles I overtook the Indian. He had got close to the mountain, and had two arrows left, which he turned loose at me. One of them cut my coat collar. I saw he had no more, rode within a rod of him, and bursted a cap at him. I then made a drive for him on my horse. He was the largest Indian I ever saw, and ran like a scared wolf. I caught my gun by the breech, ran on him and struck him over the head with such a force I broke the gun off at the breech. The barrel fell some ten feet off, and the Indian in front of me, and my horse fell over him. I lit on my feet, jumped and caught up the gun-barrel, and wheeled for the Indian. He was getting up when I hit him again over the head, killing him instantly, the blow bending the heavy barrel four inches. I jerked off his scalp and went back as fast as my horse could carry me.

On the bluff of the river sat Doc. Ripley on his horse, over an Indian he said he had killed. Said he to me: "Captain, take off his scalp for me, as your hands are bloody. I am not spleeny about such things. I have cut up many a dead person in the dissecting rooms." I dismounted, caught him by the top of his head, and as soon as I began to cut, he jumped straight on his feet. I stabbed him with my knife a few times, which soon ended him.

On examination we found he was only shot through the flesh of the arm. We counted forty-six killed. Two of our men got shot in the legs, and one in the thumb. All got well by the time we got to California. After this we traveled unmolested.

When we got on Carson River, a lamentable circumstance took place. The Kit Carson man got killed. He was the best man I had. His name was John Watson. He was killed by the worst man I had, a man who was said to be running away from Missouri for murdering a man there. They had a quarrel, and this man undertook to shoot Watson, but would have got killed if I had not interfered. Watson came to me and told me he knew the man intended killing him, and thought it hard I would not let him shoot him. I then went and talked to the man, and he promised faithfully he would not touch Watson. I told Watson there was no danger. He thought different, but said he would be quiet, and not another word passed between them. That evening Watson was lying on his blankets, sleeping, when this man, Hensley, went and put his pistol to his head and blew out his brains.

I was then out after the horses. When I came to camp he was walking around with four pistols on his belt, swearing there was not men enough in camp to take him, and if they undertook it he could kill half a dozen. I thought of taking my gun and shooting him down, but thought of my position, sat down at my camp-fire and said nothing, but thought there was time enough to have him attended to, knowing there was no show for him to get away.

The next morning we made a coffin of a wagon-box, and buried Watson in a military style, firing thirty shots over his grave. Now I will here say this man Hensley in an Indian fight was not brave, but always behind in dangerous places; although from report he had killed several men before this. I told the boys we would attend to him that evening. We wanted to move on about ten miles to get good feed for our animals. The camp, which had been almost universally lively and full of fun, moved off with a dismal look, not a cheerful countenance to be seen. It seemed as if all had lost a brother,

"I rode up by his side and shot him through the heart." Page 94

and indeed it was almost so. Watson's piercing eye had passed nothing unnoticed in our travels. He was always ahead when a fight was on hand, and when in camp would amuse the boys by telling his adventures with Kit Carson, his hunting and Indian stories, narrow escapes and big victories, which was done in such a hearty, plain, and sociable manner that everybody liked him.

We moved on, found good grass, and encamped, and soon a company of sixteen men came on the same flat, from California, and encamped below us. I went and found their captain, a man I had known in Illinois. He had been in California two years, and was going back on the forty-mile sand desert, which we had just crossed, for wagons that had been left there. I got a good drink of brandy, and then told him of the circumstance that had happened in our camp. He and all his men shouted: "Hang him up. Why have you not done it before? We have to do it in this country and in California in the absence of law. If he had done such a deed in the mines, where you are going, he would have been hung in less than three hours."

I invited the captain to come up after dark, and bring half a dozen of his best men with him, stating that I would have him arrested, and we would investigate the case. I selected four of my best men, told them to get as close to him as they could, and then bounce upon him. I watched, and he did not appear to notice until one of them got in about ten feet of him, when he straightened up, put his hand on a pistol, but had no time to draw it before all four of my men had him tight, and he was soon tied. Supper being over, the captain of the California company, with six men, came into camp. I called my company together and took a vote of the company to see what was their wish. All voted for a trial. I then appointed a judge and three jurymen, and the California captain appointed three of his men as jurymen, to hear the case. I stated that I would appoint this California captain to prosecute the case, and the prisoner might choose one or two to assist him. I took a vote on this, and it was unanimously agreed to. The prisoner got his counsel.

The judge and jury were seated, all things went off smoothly, and no evidence was denied. When through, the prisoner was asked what he had to say. He answered: "That d—d s—n of a b—h, he insulted me by giving me the lie, and no man can do that and live. That's my motto, and Watson knew it; consequently he deserved death." This was his only reason for killing him. The jury was out about fifteen minutes, and returned a verdict of murder in the first degree.

All was still, and I called a vote of the company, giving that same jury power to say what should be done with him. All agreed. They were out about five minutes, returned, and said: "Hang him." Men were sent to find a tree with a limb suitable, and found one a few hundred yards from camp. This was about two o'clock in the night. A brush-fire was built, and the prisoner notified he had half an hour to live, and could say what he had to say during that time. He got a man to pray for him, who prayed about ten minutes. Then the prisoner commenced finding fault with almost everyone in camp. His time was cried every five minutes. He swore and used the roughest language, acting more like a devil than a man going to die.

When the last five minutes was cried, he turned to me, whom he seemed to have missed in his volley of abuse, and said: "There is the captain, a man I thought was a gentleman. It was in his power to have saved me, but he has let all this go on and not tried to prevent my being hanged, and, if there is such a thing, I will come back and haunt you all the days of your life." I replied: "I am not much afraid of live men, and much less of dead ones."

A lariat was put around his neck, thrown over a limb, and he was drawn four feet from the ground, and the other end fastened to a stake, and left until morning. Next morning he was rolled in his blanket, and buried under the same tree, and at eight o'clock we rolled on. I noticed the looks of the company that day, and all seemed to say we had done right.

Next we got to the Mormon station kept by Colonel Reese, a Mormon trader. It is now known as Genoa. There were eight or ten men there, but not a woman in the valley. When we reached California I sold my stock and went to mining; worked in the Coon Hill diggings four or five weeks, and sank three hundred dollars. This was one mile south of Placerville, then called Hangtown.

While working there, William Haven, a man who had

wintered in Salt Lake Valley the year before, came to see me and wanted me to mine with him. He was in company with two others, he having two shares and they one apiece; so I went and paid him two hundred dollars for one of his shares, and went to work. I soon made acquaintances, and to many was a matter of curiosity as a Mormon from Salt Lake. People would come to see me, as if expecting to see a different species of human being. Sometimes we made as high as forty dollars per day to the hand.

There was no law in the mines at that time only miners' laws, which was justice in all cases, irrespective of persons. I had to sit arbitrator on two cases of theft, the punishment for which was hanging. Both were for stealing money, small amounts, not over one hundred dollars. After sentence, I made a speech begging leniency—asked mercy for them—proposed giving them a good dose of pine limbs, which, when put to a vote of the company, was agreed to. They got a good dressing-down, and were never seen on that flat afterwards.

I made about one thousand dollars there, went to another place and sank money running a tunnel; went to another place and began placer mining again.

About this time the California papers were full of news about trouble in Utah. Some judges had been sent here, and they and Brother Brigham could not hitch horses. The papers talked fight all the time, and stated that United States troops were to be sent to Salt Lake as soon as they could cross the Plains. I grew uneasy about home, and determined to return as soon as I could cross the mountains. I had intended to stay another year, but, true to my friend Brigham, thought if trouble came on I could help him some, and this was more than money to me.

I had the pleasure of digging gold in several places. The largest nugget I found weighed a little over four ounces, but I worked many a day that I did not make anything. I invested money in deep diggings, and lost several hundred dollars. In June, '52, eight of us were ready to go to Salt Lake, four of us living there, and the other four going to the States. We bought Spanish horses and mules, fine and fat, rigged up pack-saddles, bought good riding-saddles, and set out for Salt Lake, which we reached in twenty-one days. On the Humboldt River, where the Indians had been so bad the year before, we met a heavy emigration going to California, this—1852—being the greatest year for emigration.

We arrived in Salt Lake the 3d of July. I went home, ten miles south of the city; found the family all alive and well, the stock all fat, and I at home again with a few hundreds to make them comfortable. The next day I went and saw Brigham Young, and made him a present of fifty dollars. We had a long meeting.

I spent the summer and fall at home, trading some with the late California emigrants, getting two poor animals for one fat one, and bought some at less than half what they were worth when fat.

Winter came on and there was much said about one Ike Hatch and his company stealing horses and cattle. Brigham wanted me to watch him and some others, and report to him, which I did for two or three months. I found that he was killing beef and bringing it to town, and stealing horses and trading them off to persons going away from the Territory. He was bringing in beef for some of Brigham Young's special friends, either as a donation or partnership; anyway they had him steal for them, and bring it to them. I reported this to Brigham also, which seemed to strike him anew with rather a set-back, and I was not asked to watch him again. A month or two after this a man living thirty-five miles south, who had lost his last and only pair of horses, found out Hatch had stolen them, came to me and said he had got the word from Brigham to kill him, and wanted me and another man to assist him. Hatch was watched for and shot, lived a few days and died. This was laid to me, and I never denied it. Brigham Young said that was a good deed, let who would do it.

After he was killed, his family moved south fifty miles, but his comrades kept up their stealing, and finally started East. This man who had lost his horses came to me about midnight the first of April, '53, and said the Hatch party had gone, and he thought they had his horses along, from what he could learn; said he had been to Brigham Young, and he told him to come and get me and some others, and follow and kill the last one of them.

The next day I was in the city, mounted on the best horse in the Territory, with another good one for my friend. We got off at 3 p. m. The day had been warm, the snow deep, and the waters were high; so that we had to travel on the mountain sides, on the Indian trail, up the cañon. The wind blew a hurricane blast, and the clouds overshadowed the mountain, so that when we had passed the first range we were obliged to stop. It commenced to snow, and one of the worst storms I ever saw ensued. Morning came and the storm abated, but the tracks of the party we were in pursuit of were put out by the snow. Guessing at the road they would go, we set out and went to Fort Bridger, but could hear nothing of them. I was left at Fort Bridger with one man to watch for them. The balance went to Green River, seventy miles farther on. They had been gone two days, when some mountaineers came to Fort Bridger and told me they had seen such men as we were inquiring for in Echo Cañon the day before, and when they—*i. e.,* the horse-thieves, saw them, they ran, taking up the mountain. I had only a boy of eighteen with me, untried and unproven; did not know whether he would stand up to the rack in danger or not. I asked him what he thought of going after them, and he said he would go with me.

We started at 10 o'clock a. m., and by dark were at the mouth of Echo Cañon, seventy miles away, where an old man and his son-in-law lived. But these were of no advantage to us, as neither of them had nerve enough to pull a setting-hen off her nest. I inquired about the thieves, but they knew nothing about them. It commenced snowing and raining that night, and kept it up until the next day. Next morning it cleared off fine and warm; the snow passed off the south hill-sides, and we went out to look for tracks. Found old ones on the mountain-side which we thought must have been made by them; followed them about four miles and came to fresh ones, just made, going towards Weber River. We looked up and down the river, being on the mountain-side, so we could see for miles each way, and saw them near the river about two miles off. Saw them shooting wild geese. There were four of them, and all had guns and pistols. We had Colt's revolvers only.

We watched them some time, and studied how we could get to them without being seen. We fell back and took down the river, keeping out of sight until we were close to them. I told Joe to cock his pistol, and I cocked mine. I looked at him, and he was pale and trembling. I hit him a slap on the face, and told him I would break his head if he did not look out. His color came, his nerve steadied, and his eyes flashed with anger. I said to him: "Obey orders, and follow me."

We rode around the brush and made a dash upon them, at the same time crying out: "Here they are, boys, come on." I ordered a surrender, told them to deliver their arms to Joe forthwith, at the same time presenting my pistol at the one I considered the most dangerous, and swearing to shoot the first man that hesitated. They delivered up their arms in quick time. I told Joe to keep back a few paces, while I marched them in front of me to the house at the mouth of the cañon. When we got into the road they wanted to know where the balance of the company was. I made them believe they were close by, but when we got to the house it was soon known that we had no company with us. They swore if they had known that, they would not have been taken, and began talking of leaving. We took a gun apiece, hid the balance of their arms, and stood guard over them.

In a short time our men were up, not a dry hair on their horses. When they returned to Fort Bridger and heard the news, they came on as fast as their horses could bring them. We then learned the thieves' camp was six miles back in the mountain; that their horses were there, and all their camp equipage, and that one of their company had gone to the city for flour.

The next day we went to their camp and brought everything to the house; found three stolen animals, but the man who had come for me, expecting to find his horses, was disappointed. We had no evidence against three of the prisoners, but started them for the city, and sent the guilty one down the river with a bullet-hole through him.

We divided our company, as there were two roads to the city, in order to catch the other thief, Ike Vaughn. The party I was not with caught him at the mouth of Emigration Cañon, within five miles of the city, returning to his company. I got to the city with my party about dark, and learned they had Vaughn. We had had a hard trip through the snow, crossing the mountain, had storms on us half the time, and were tired and worn out, so we turned the prisoner over to the acting police, with instructions to wind up his career that night.

About midnight we were wakened from a sound sleep

by one of the police, who told us the prisoner was gone. We asked him how it happened. He said they took him out and hit him a rap on the head, when he broke loose and outran them. We got up and searched until daylight, but got no trace of him. I went with Mr. R——, the man who had lost his horses, to see Brigham Young, and make a report of what we had done.

Mr. R—— gave him a full report of all that had taken place, and the escape of Vaughn. He said we had done well; told us to go home and rest, and then go after Vaughn again, and never stop until we had killed him. We then asked him what should be done with their property. He said: "Turn it over to the Church." He saw Mr. R—— did not like this, having lost his horses, which were taken by this party, been on a hard trip, and then to turn over property to those who had plenty, did not suit him. Brother Brigham finally said: "Take the property and divide it among yourselves," which we did.

I got a small Spanish mule worth seventy-five dollars, a rifle, and two half-worn blankets for my share. Here let me say that this is all I ever got for services rendered on Brigham Young's orders. Neither did I ever receive a present from him, not so much as one dollar. But from the cause of my former belief I questioned nothing, supposing him right in all things, and it not only a duty, but highly necessary that I should obey his commands, and in the end it would prove both spiritual and temporal salvation to me, which situation thousands of others are now in, in this Territory.

We rested one day, when Mr. R——, with one man, started south to San Pete Valley, a distance of one hundred and twenty-five miles, to see if Vaughn was there, as he had some acquaintances living there. They called on the widow of I. Hatch, thinking he might be there, but got no news of him. Mrs. Hatch told Mr. R—— that her husband said just before he died that he had taken Mr. R——'s horses, and sold them to a Californian; that they were gone and he was sorry, but could not help it now, and wanted her to tell Mr. R——, if she ever saw him.

They returned, not hearing of Vaughn, but said they had things fixed so that if he was seen he would be attended to. Shortly after this he told me Vaughn was caught and killed down South. I never asked him who did it; nor do I know yet. The other three were turned loose, and went to California.

I had been making preparations for a road trade all winter, intending to take an outfit and go somewhere in the vicinity of Green River, and trade with the California and Oregon immigration for tired and lame stock, and buy surplus loading, which was generally sold cheap when teams began to get tired.

I commenced reading law, of which I had a smattering when quite young. I had given attention to it ever since I saw that law knowledge and talent were quite ordinary, as a general thing, in this country. I thought I would, after awhile, make a business of practicing law, but this summer I intended to trade. I got my outfit of stock, groceries, and a set of blacksmith's tools, and

Hickman killing Hartley, by order of Orson Hyde, one of the Twelve Apostles. Page 98.

went to Green River; got there the first of May, and the mountain-traders, some forty or fifty, all met me, wanting whisky. I had plenty, and sold whisky a few days at two dollars per pint, and took in six or seven hundred dollars. I thought I had better go back farther on the road, as there were so many trading at and around Green River; so I went to Pacific Springs, sixty miles farther east, set up shop and grocery, and the immigration soon began to come. Horse-shoeing, wagon-repairing, and whisky were all in big demand, and lame stock cheap.

I had been there but a few days when Doc. Morton, from St. Louis, came with a similar outfit for a road trade. He was surgeon in Colonel Doniphan's regiment of volunteers, from western Missouri, during the Mexican war. He was also the Morton of the wholesale drug store in St. Louis. This gentleman had seen something of the Plains, and was taking this trip for a change, not expecting to find any trader there. He seemed sad and disappointed. I saw he was a gentleman, and told him there would be trade enough for us both; so he set up his establishment about two hundred yards from me. Emigration from the East to California and Oregon soon came thick. Drove after drove of cattle passed daily, most of which had lame or tired ones to sell. We paid from five to ten dollars per head; seldom over. Traded for several good horses, some lame, some sick; bought clothing, groceries, wagons, harness, and tents at a low figure.

We wound up some time in August. The Doctor went

to Salt Lake with his stock, sold out, and went to St. Louis that fall. I got home with over a hundred head more stock than I started with, and a little of almost everything else. I made a reckoning after I got home of what I had made that summer, and it was over nine thousand dollars. I had bought some of the finest Durham stock I ever saw; they being heavy and tender, could not be driven through. From this stock I raised, and had the premium stock of the Salt Lake fairs for many years.

During the summer a difficulty took place between the ferrymen and mountain men. The latter had always owned and run the ferry across Green River; but the Utah Legislature granted a charter to Hawley, Thompson & McDonald, for all the ferries there. The mountain men, who had lived there for many years, claimed their rights to be the oldest, and a difficulty took place, in which the mountain men took forcible possession of all the ferries but one, making some thirty thousand dollars out of them. When the ferrying season was over, the party having the charter brought suit against them for all they had made during the summer.

About this time it was rumored that Jim Bridger was furnishing the Indians with powder and lead to kill Mormons. Affidavits were made to that effect, and the sheriff was ordered out with a *posse* of one hundred and fifty men to arrest him, capture his ammunition, and destroy all his liquors. I was sent for to come to Brigham Young's office. He told me he wanted me to go with the sheriff, James Ferguson, and party, as I had been out there that summer, was acquainted with those mountaineers, and might be of special service. I accordingly went; Bridger had heard of this and left—no one knew where to. We searched around several days for him. Finally one of the party who had taken the ferries, came to Fort Bridger and was arrested. No ammunition was found, but the whisky and rum, of which he had a good stock, was destroyed by doses: the sheriff, most of his officers, the doctor and chaplain of the company, all aided in carrying out the orders, and worked so hard day and night that they were exhausted —not being able to stand up. But the privates, poor fellows! were rationed, and did not do so much.

I saw how things were going, and told the sheriff I was going home. He then asked me if I would make one of Lieutenant Eph. Hanks' party to take the prisoner into Salt Lake. I agreed, and we started in the afternoon. Hanks was full of rum. The necessary supplies were laid in, which consisted of a few canteens of the same. We intended to travel forty miles before we slept, but when night came on it was very dark. The canteens made things lively until we came to some brush, when the prisoner, Elisha Ryan, slipped off his horse, and in an instant was in the brush out of sight. We searched for him an hour or two, and sent two of the party back to Fort Bridger, while Hanks and myself came on to the city and made our report. Hanks being one of the star boys, so looked up to, felt rather cheap when his rum gave out and he came to himself, on seeing what he had done.

The *posse* went to Green River, shot two or three mountaineers, took several hundred head of stock, returned to Fort Bridger, and what whisky they could not drink they poured out, reserving, however, enough to keep them drunk until they got home. The property that was taken went to pay a few officers, and, as was said, the expenses of the *posse;* but, poor fellows, I never knew of one of them getting a dollar. It went to pay tithing; and, finally, all was gobbled up and turned over to the Church, and Hawley & Co. never got a cent. This did not suit him very well; but he had to stand it, and it sticks in his craw to this day. The old man tells some wonderful stories about that and other losses sustained by Church authority; but that is his history and not mine, and I will pass over it as I have, and will do, with many others; but, at the close of my history, I may give to you the manner in which several have been treated in financial affairs by those holding authority over them.

That fall, after harvest, my horses were gathered and put into a field having probably seventy-five acres, which had not been cultivated, and bore the finest of grass. One morning my hired boy came in and told me Frenchy was gone, one of the finest little French horses I ever saw; his mane hanging to his knees, and his foretop to the end of his nose; a horse I had got the year before, and given a big price for him. I found him very gentle, and made my wife a present of him—that same good woman whom I have told you I courted and married when but a boy. He paced finely; she loved horseback riding, and with him could make a showing among a hundred horses.

We found where the fence had been let down and the horse led out, and a man's tracks. I sent for my horse, which was the best in the Territory, and put one of my hired men on the next best, and started. About noon we got his track, and were satisfied which way he had gone. We traveled at the rate of eight miles an hour, and just before sundown I saw my horse coming out of the swamps of Utah Lake, sixty miles from where we started. I was both mad and tired. The man on him hailed me and wanted to know if he could have our company south. I felt too indignant to speak. I rode up by his side and shot him through the head, took my horse and went home. I did not get off my horse to examine him. I never heard from him after. Whether he was found or buried I do not know.

I was in the city a few days after, and, as in duty bound, made report to Brigham Young, who held the right of life-taking in his own hands, and nobody else, as we had often been told. He said I had done just right. I will here state that, while at Pacific Springs, on the South Pass, at my trading-post, among the emigration passing, one of my brothers came along, going to California. I had not seen him for twelve years, and did not know him. He had studied medicine, had his diploma, and was going to California to practice his profession. I, with much persuasion, got him to stop and spend the winter with me; but before the winter was over, we Mormonized him and got him to join the

Church. He has been here ever since, and is a good Mormon; but, poor fellow, he has never had but one wife, won't practice medicine, lives on his farm, raises grain, attends to his stock, and goes along as though he was a stereotyped Christian indeed.

I spent the most of my time that winter reading law-books. I also got the appointment of Deputy United States marshal under Marshal Joseph L. Heywood, he having been appointed by President Z. Taylor, which office I held until '58, doing most of the Marshal's business in the courts, and making all arrests of hard men. That winter, while Judge Shaffer's court was in session, I made application for license to practice law, and a committee, with Almon W. Babbitt as foreman, was appointed to examine me. I was in attendance at the court acting as marshal and bailiff at the same time. The committee reported next morning favorable, after giving me what I thought was a pretty rigid examination, and I was licensed.

That winter a new county was granted by the Legislature, taking in Green River Ferry, called Green River County. W. I. Appleby was appointed probate judge, with power to organize said county and appoint all necessry officers, who were to hold office until the next election.* From the time that those mountain men had had their property taken by the sheriff and his *posse,* very ill feelings had existed. Threats were made that they would have as much property out of the Mormons as they had lost by them. Some fears were entertained

*See Appendix—B.

that they might bother the emigration the next fall, and Brigham Young wanted me to go and stay on Green River that summer, and, if possible, quiet them down in some way or other; and if I could not make peace with them any other way, pitch in and kill those that would not come to terms without, and especially Ryan (he was with the Indians, and would do us much harm, and must go up). This being my charge, I set out with Judge Appleby and Rev. Orson Hyde, who had charge of the new settlement, Fort Supply, twelve miles south of Fort Bridger. Our company consisted of fifteen, this being about the first of May, '54, as soon as we could get across the mountains for snow.

Orson Hyde being the head of The Twelve, obedience was required to his commands, in the absence of Brigham Young, in all things, whether spiritual or temporal; and, in fact, the man who did not obey had better leave when he could, especially those who might refuse, or give any intimation of a dislike to things that elsewhere would be an open violation of law. But the satisfied point and undoubted fact that God had established His kingdom in the mountains, and Brigham was conversant with the Almighty, was a settled question. In all candor I say I do not think there was then in Utah one in fifty, or, I might say, one in a hundred, who did not believe it. This man Orson Hyde was sanguine in this belief, although there were some points in Brigham Young's conduct he could not see through, but attributed it all, he said, to his inability to comprehend the ways of the Almighty. I have traveled with and talked to him on all these subjects.

When we had got across what was known as the Big Mountain, and into East Cañon, some three or four miles, one Mr. Hartley came to us from Provo City. This Hartley was a young lawyer who had come to Salt Lake from Oregon the fall before, and had married a Miss Bullock, of Provo, a respectable lady of a good family. But word had come to Salt Lake (so said, I never knew whether it did or not), that he had been engaged in some counterfeiting affair. He was a fine-looking, intelligent young man. He told me he had never worked any in his life, and was going to Fort Bridger or Green River to see if he could not get a job of clerking, or something that he could do. But previous to this, at the April Conference, Brigham Young, before the congregation, gave him a tremendous blowing up, calling him all sorts of bad names, and saying he ought to have his throat cut, which made him feel very bad. He declared he was not guilty of the charges.

I saw Orson Hyde looking very sour at him, and after he had been in camp an hour or two, Hyde told me that he had orders from Brigham Young, if he came to Fort Supply to have him used up. "Now," said he, "I want you and George Boyd to do it." I saw him and Boyd talking together; then Boyd came to me and said: "It's all right, Bill; I will help you to kill that fellow." One of our teams was two or three miles behind, and Orson Hyde wished me to go back and see if anything had happened to it. Boyd saddled his horse to go with me, but

Hartley stepped up and said he would go if Boyd would let him have his horse. Orson Hyde said: "Let him have your horse," which Boyd did. Orson Hyde then whispered to me: "Now is your time; don't let him come back." We started, and about half a mile on had to cross the cañon stream, which was midsides to our horses. While crossing, Hartley got a shot and fell dead in the creek. His horse took fright and ran back to camp.

I went on and met Hosea Stout, who told me the team was coming close by. I turned back, Stout with me, for our camp. Stout asked me if I had seen that fellow, meaning Hartley. I told him he had come to our camp, and he said from what he had heard he ought to be killed. I then told him all that had happened, and he said that was good. When I returned to camp Boyd told me that his horse came into camp with blood on the saddle, and he and some of the boys took it to the creek and washed it off. Orson Hyde told me that was well done; that he and some others had gone on the side of the mountain, and seen the whole performance. We hitched up and went to Weber River that day. When supper was over, Orson Hyde called all the camp together, and said he wanted a strong guard on that night, for that fellow that had come to us in the forenoon had left the company; he was a bad man, and it was his opinion that he intended stealing horses that night. This was about as good a take-off as he could get up, it was all nonsense; it would do well enough to tell; as everyone that did not know what had happened believed it.*

*See Appendix—C.

Hanging Rock, Echo Cañon; near where Hickman, with his prisoner, Yates, was met by Joseph A. Young, who said his father wanted Yates killed. Page 124.

CHAPTER IV.

FROM 1854 TO 1858.

GREEN RIVER COUNTY ORGANIZED—HICKMAN APPOINTED SHERIFF, PROSECUTING ATTORNEY, ASSESSOR, AND COLLECTOR—RYAN RE-ARRESTED, PARDONED, AND BECOMES A FRIEND OF HICKMAN— HIS MURDER—BRIGHAM'S MEANNESS IN BUSINESS—COL. STEPTOE'S ARRIVAL—GRAND PROSPECTING TOUR—FREMONT'S PEAK, OR FREMONT'S HOAX?—ARREST OF CARLOS MURRAY—HICKMAN ELECTED TO THE LEGISLATURE—DISGRACEFUL CONDUCT OF JUDGE DRUMMOND—THE "MORMON BOYS" TRAP HIM INTO A FIX—HICKMAN RETURNS TO MISSOURI FOR THE MAIL AND EXPRESS COMPANY—MUTTERINGS OF WAR—HICKMAN RIDES FIVE HUNDRED MILES IN SIX DAYS—THE MORMON WAR BEGUN—MORMON TACTICS—BURNING GOVERNMENT TRAINS—HICKMAN AS A GUERRILLA CAPTAIN.

We went on to Fort Supply, where the county was organized by Judge Appleby, and the officers appointed, sworn in, and commissioned by him to hold until the August election. He had special instructions from Brigham Young to appoint me sheriff, in order to give me power over the mountaineers, which was agreeable to the Judge, as we were always good friends. The Judge loaded me down with offices. I had the office of sheriff

and county prosecuting attorney, assessor and collector.*
After this was through with, we moved to Green River,
opened our offices, and were ready for business. These
offices were not desired by me, for I knew I could go
back to South Pass, and make more money at my old
stand than I could at Green River with all these offices;
but I had to obey counsel. My services were needed
there, and I then dared not refuse. I got my brother,
who had come on the year before, to go to South Pass
and attend to my business for me, making him my full
partner. He did tolerable well for us both, but nothing like I had done the year before.

The mountaineers began to gather in, the quiet ones,
such as Jack Robinson, the well-known old mountaineer.
He said he was glad I was going to stop on Green River;
glad the county was organized, and we had an officer to
keep peace; hoped things would go off quiet that year.
I took a great deal of pains to get his confidence, knowing he was an influential man among them, which I
soon got. I found him a fine, clever old man, and the
best of feelings have existed between us ever since. I
had not been on Green River long before I had a difficulty with a half-breed Delaware Indian, considered a
very dangerous man, and conquered, but did not kill
him. This gave me much influence. The other Indians
thought I was a great war-chief that feared nothing,
and a medicine man, too.

I will here tell you their fanatical notions about what
they call a medicine man. They firmly believe Shinab

*See Appendix—D.

—that is, the sun, makes and keeps men from being hit with ball or arrow. The chiefs keep their men in dread and fear, telling them they can't be killed. I saw a chief once strip himself and walk through an Indian village, inviting anyone that wished to take a shot at him, but no one dared do it, believing that he could not be killed, and if they shot and missed him he might be mad and kill them. Their come off to this is, in case one of their medicine men get killed, they say he was no medicine man, but had lied to them about it. But so long as he lives, it is all well enough.

The different bands of Indians kept coming in, who had had their minds soured by the mountaineers in conscquence of the Mormons taking away the rights of their friends. Those men told them that was their country, and they had a right to say who should stay in it, or who should run the ferries. I got Uncle Jack Robinson* to explain to them how things were, and what laws and organizations had been extended over that country; that it was not to take their country nor deprive them of their rights, but it was done to make the white men do right while passing through their country, and this authority had come from the Great Father at Washington. He at the same time told them I was the chief to make all white men behave, which gave them entire satisfaction. After making them some presents, such as

* An old mountaineer with two Indian wives, who has lived on Green River for thirty years.

a beef, a few sacks of flour, and some sugar and coffee, they all left satisfied, and have never made any trouble there since.

Some few weeks after this, Ryan and a party of half-a-dozen came from Wind River, took possession of the ferry, and commenced running it, crossing the emigration, and taking in the pay. The owners came to Judge Appleby's office, scared half to death, having been run off and heavily threatened, supposing he (Ryan) would have enough help to hold the ferry, and that would be an end of their ferrying that year. A writ was soon issued for the arrest of Ryan. I selected two good men to go ahead of me and be with Ryan to keep him from getting the bulge on me. They were strangers to him. I told them I would be there alone an hour after. They went, and I soon followed. My policy was to take the bulge on and fasten him, and by that the balance of his party would weaken. This worked well.

When I got in sight I rode up at half speed alone, no one thinking I would dare undertake any arrest without a *posse*. I dismounted, and with a cocked revolver in my hand, ordered Ryan not to move, telling him he was my prisoner, and ordered his hands tied behind. This was the first of my two men being known. They tied him in quick time, while I held my revolver at his breast. His men stood looking on in astonishment. I watched them closely, and told them if they kept still they would be all right, but if they did not I would shoot the last one of them. I mounted Ryan on his horse, one of my men leading him and two of us behind. It was all done in three minutes, and we were off at high speed.

When we had got about half-way to camp, I looked at him and saw he was a different man from what he was represented to be, and I told the boys to loose him. We got into conversation, and he expressed himself freely to me. He had supposed that the ferry company had got all his property, amounting to ten or twelve thousand dollars, and he was left poor. He said if they had to refund the money they had taken in the year before, it should have been on all the owners in the ferry, and not on him alone, and he had sworn to have satisfaction in some way. He seemed honest in his conclusions. I then told him how his property was taken and what was done with it, with the exception of the church part. Those sacred things were kept sacred from him. This was the first time he knew how his property had gone, and made a change in his feelings. He stopped just before we got to the door of the court-room, and said to me, "Get me out of this and I will do just as you say hereafter." I answered: "Good, my boy, there shall not a hair of your head be hurt." He said his men would be uneasy about him, and he must go back that night. He promised to be back in the morning if I would allow him to go. I asked him if he would turn over the ferry to the owners, and he said he would.

I saw the Judge, made my return on the writ, and told him the prisoner would not be ready for trial until the next day. He answered, "Very well, he is in your custody; he can have until to-morrow at ten o'clock A.M., at

which time you will have him before the court." I told
Ryan to go and give up the ferry, and be back by that
time, telling him I thought him a man of his word, and
would trust him, but if he did not come it would break
me of my office and subject me to a heavy fine; that I
was doing this on my own responsibility. After he was
gone I was reprimanded by nearly all for letting him go.
Bottles of whisky and champagne were bet on his not
coming back. I took all the bets, some dozen bottles in
all. Before 9 A.M., he was there with four of his friends,
seemed pleased to see me, and proposed taking a drink.
I told him I had made our whiskey for the day betting
on him. "Well," said he, "that's good; take all such bets
when I give my word." I saw the prosecuting parties,
who were willing, after hearing his story, to withdraw the
case, and told him they would pay the costs if he would
let them alone. He promised them he would, and to
their astonishment pulled out the money he had taken
in and handed it over to them. They gave him back two
hundred dollars, which he reluctantly took, saying if he
was not so poor he would not have it.

Ryan took a liking to me, and ever after was a special
friend of mine. He was of great service to me as Indian
interpreter, as he could talk the Indian language as well
as they could. He came home with me and staid that
winter. I had him with me on three trips to the Indians,
as per order of Brigham Young, Superintendent of Indian affairs; while he held that office under appointment
of President Filmore. We had one starving trip through
our foolishness. We were sent by Brigham Young to

hunt up and invite in Washakie, a Shoshone chief, and his band of Indians. We went to Green River, and heard those Indians were up on head waters; so we concluded to make an Indian march, and not take any provisions with us, not even so much as salt. We had one white man and two Indians, five in all. We traveled eight days and found no Indians; had, during this time, two small ducks not much larger than a man's fist, and four mountain trout, which would probably weigh three-fourths of a pound each. This was all we had, except a few rosebuds, until the eighth day, just at sundown, one of the Indians killed a large antelope. We were within fifteen miles of Fort Bridger, where we expected to get our supper that night; but this antelope was too good a thing. We stripped off our saddles and went to roasting, and did not stop until it was all eaten. We then lay down and slept as sweetly as children in their mother's arms. The game had all left the country we were traveling in, and there was not so much as a prairie chicken to be seen.

Ryan, poor fellow, went to Fort Bridger early in the spring, before I did, and got killed by a Spaniard, who, without cause, slipped upon him and shot him, and then left the country. When Ryan first came to the city he went to see Brigham Young, and told him his situation and how he had been treated. Brigham promised him an interest in the ferries the next year, and told him he would give him a chance to get his money back. He then asked Brigham to lend him five hundred or a thousand dollars until the next summer. Brigham told him he did not have it, but turned to me and told me to go and borrow him what money he wanted. I borrowed seven hundred and fifty dollars and gave to him, which, after his death, I had to pay. I spoke to Brigham Young about it, and he said I must pay it, and be more cautious hereafter whom I borrowed money for. I thought I would, at his suggestion anyhow.

In the fall of 1854, Col. E. J. Steptoe came to Salt Lake City with three hundred United States troops, and wintered in the city. They got along peaceably until Christmas day, when a portion of them and a good many citizens got drunk.. They had a regular street fight, and there were a good many sore heads and bloody noses on both sides. But the officers put a stop to this, and all was quiet the next day. I got in town just in time to see the crowd dispersing. In the spring, Col. Steptoe went to California with his troops, taking with him O. P. Rockwell as guide.

That winter Judge Shaffer died, and Judge Kinney took his place, being appointed Chief Justice for Utah. The Judge was merchandising, keeping hotel, and holding court in Salt Lake City, all at the same time. In the spring of '55 I bought a fourth interest in the ferries; went to Green River, repaired the boats, and got the ferries in running condition. We heard the emigration for California and Oregon would be small, and would not be along until late in the season; so, in company with others who had come in that country to trade, and some of my hired men, I agreed to take a prospecting tour on Sweet Water, South Pass, and Wind River.

Seven of us rigged up with pack animals for a three or four week's trip. Myself and one other, having worked in the California diggings, were the only ones that knew anything of gold hunting. We spent a week prospecting a stream where rich gold quartz is now found, and mills crushing it. We found gold on all those streams, but not in paying quantities. We did not find any place that we thought would pay more than two dollars a day to the man. We knew nothing about quartz mining, consequently did not hunt for lodes.

After searching on Strawberry Creek, Willow Creek, and many of their tributaries, we went into the high mountains, finding lakes almost on the tops, and immense snow-beds. We got several hundred feet higher than the Fremont Peak, so much talked of several years ago; a statement having been published that Col. Fremont had stopped and bleed himself twice before reaching the summit. This, like many other stories of adventurers in these mountains, is all a hoax. We had no trouble in breathing, being so high above, and the distance together, that what is called Fremont's Peak looked like nothing more than a common mound or butte.

Now, some may say we were mistaken, for Fremont's Peak is the highest mountain in all North America. This is not so. I have been with mountaineers who showed me that mountain, who were with Fremont, and laughed at the ridiculous story told and published about Fremont Peak. We crossed the high mountain of which I have been writing, and struck the head waters of Wind River on the north side of it. Here I saw more game

Hickman killing Yates, by order of Brigham Young.—Hosea Stout holding the lantern. Page 125.

than I ever had seen at one place—buffalo, elk, deer, antelope, and bear were all to be seen at once. We killed all we wanted, and had some great sport after them, especially the bear, sometimes shooting a dozen balls into one before producing death.

We ran over the whole country, found but little gold, and were ready for a return, when one evening we saw two Indians coming. We saw them ten miles off, and got ahead of them; found them to be Snake Indians whom I knew. They told me the Blackfeet Indians were coming, and we had better leave quick. We left the next morning, passing around the Wind River mountain on the east; went to Sweet Water; spent two or three days, and left for Green River, believing, from finding gold in so many places, that some time there would be gold found in that country in paying quantities. Reached Green River, and no emigration yet, so I left the ferry in charge of good men and went home; stayed a few days, and made arrangements for the August elections. We then went back, closed up our ferrying, went to Fort Supply, and remained until the first Monday in August.

I was then elected representative of the county. The Territorial Legislature then met at Filmore, one hundred and fifty miles south of Salt Lake City. I went to Salt Lake City again, and attended to several law-suits in the Probate and District courts. The grand jury of the United States District Court found an indictment against Carlos Murray for murder—the unlawful killing of an Indian—and the writ was put in my hand for his arrest. He lived on the Humboldt River, four hundred miles from here in a wild Indian country. The court allowed me a *posse* of forty men. We went, found, arrested, and brought Murray to Salt Lake City.

The legislature set, I attended and got my traveling fees for two hundred and eighty miles. I rented a room, had it furnished with the best the country afforded, dressed in the best clothes I could find, and attended forty days. I was on the committee of counties and corporations.

About this time Judge W. W. Drummond had been holding a term of the District Court, and had with him a woman whom he had picked up in Washington, leaving his wife and family, and had this prostitute sitting on the bench with him when trying a case of murder. She was writing billets and passing to him while on his judicial bench. I heard this in Salt Lake City a few days before leaving for Filmore, and made an assertion on the street that if I had a murder case before him, and he had that woman on the bench, I would kick them both out of the house. He heard this before I got to Filmore, and issued a bench warrant for my arrest for contempt of court. I heard of it when I got in town, and said if he served a writ on me I would horse-whip him. It was not served.

During the sitting of the Legislature, a Jew, by the name of Abrams, had a difficulty with him, in which Drummond threatened to kill him. The other two Judges were holding a term of the Supreme Court, and I thought this a good chance to get even with him, so I got the Jew to swear out a writ, and had him arrested.

The Jew got me to prosecute the case for him. I got another attorney to assist me, as I learned Drummond had employed two. We went into the case, and, in spite of all opposition, showed him up in his proper light. We went into his character and general course, which we made look bad enough. After working at this four days, we got the Jew to withdraw the prosecution by Drummond paying the costs. I had handled him until I was satisfied. We were never friends afterwards. He published several barefaced falsehoods about me after he went to the States.

Many of you have no doubt heard of the government officials in Utah having troubles, and some serious ones too, but this is the only one I ever had any difficulty with. I generally got along well with them, and have always tried to keep peace, and befriended some of them when in embarrassed conditions, and actually needing help from unjust proceedings against them, some of whose statements you will find in this book.

The summer previous, that is in '55, grasshoppers come into Salt Lake and many of the valleys, destroying the crops entirely, and even the grass on the benches looked as though it had been burnt, leaving nothing for stock. I took my stock to Rush Valley, to winter, where the grasshoppers had not been. I built log-houses, put up hay and made good corrals; stayed there until spring, and then moved back to my farm, ten miles south of Salt Lake City. I went to Green River that summer again, to attend the ferries and trade. The emigration was small that year, 1856, and nothing of great interest passed. Good crops were raised, and the poor, who had suffered much for want of food the year before, now had plenty.

We had some exciting lawsuits, every plug lawyer trying to excel and show his mighty talents and oratorical powers. The winter following was a very severe one. We had to take our stock from Salt Lake Valley to another valley to winter.

This winter, '56-'57, one Mr. Hiram Kimball got a contract to carry the mail from Independence, Missouri, to Salt Lake City, once a month for four years. He not being a man of much means in those days, though he had been wealthy in Nauvoo times, sought assistance from O. P. Rockwell and myself, both of us having stock to carry the mail. We agreed upon terms; Rockwell was to carry from Fort Laramie to Salt Lake, and I from Laramie to Independence. Arrangements being made, I was ready to start, although two parties had tried to get through the mountains and failed, one man having frozen to death before going twenty miles.

About this time Brighm Young and others got up a great carrying and express company, and made us put our mail interests into that company, and run together. I was sick of it, and tried to get out, but "No," said Brigham Young, "You are the very man; get your bays and roll out; you can go." I obeyed reluctantly. I dreaded the trip, knowing I would have to be gone three months or more, suffer many privations, be at a heavy expense, and the way they had things fixed, not make a dollar.

We were ten days going the first hundred and thirteen miles, to Fort Bridger, with the best of animals. We were fifteen days on the bleak desert going from Fort Bridger to South Pass. We would travel all day, tramp the snow and lead our animals, which, with great difficulty, we could get to travel very slow. At night we would camp on some knoll that the snow was blown off of, and by a poor sage brush fire cook a camp-kettle of coffee and another of corn, having got out of provisions, all but a sack of corn I had taken along to feed the horses. Several of these nights I thought I would freeze to death, but stood it better than any of the others.

We finally got through the snow into a little valley near Devil's Gate, on Sweet Water, where we found good grass for our stock, which they very much needed, having been without several days. The next morning we finished our corn, having only a scanty meal, and had not a bite of anything to eat in the company. We packed up and started for Devil's Gate, twenty miles distant, where we expected to find provisions plenty, knowing that a train of goods had been left there the fall before, under a guard of fifteen men; the snow having fallen so deep they could not reach Salt Lake City. We had not traveled far before we saw eight or ten buffalo. Two men were sent out, and soon shot a large one. We were in the center of a valley on a nice stream, where there was plenty of wood, and any quantity of the best mountain grass. We stopped, skinned and packed to camp all the meat, and the greatest eating I ever saw then took place. I cautioned the men not to eat too much; but a continual eating was kept up all day by our company, consisting of nine men. The next morning we all put all that was left of the buffalo in two flour sacks, and packed it on one mule. This is a big story, but true.

The next day we reached Devil's Gate, and found the men out of provisions; they had been living on beef hides for several days. I asked them if there was no provisions among the goods they were guarding. They said they thought there was something that would do to eat, but they dared not touch it. I told them they were foolish; to help themselves to anything there was there to eat. I told them I would be responsible and shoulder all the blame for doing this, as I wanted some provisions for my men; I would hand it out, they could take an account of it, and report to the owners that it was done by me and my party. This pleased the poor suffering fellows. We burst open the door of the cabin in which the goods were stored, and found plenty of sugar, tea, coffee, rice and dried fruit; all hands helped themselves, and we had a great general feast.

We now had bare ground to travel on, but our horses were worn out, and we could only make twenty miles per day. After forty days' travel we reached Fort Laramie. There we found Mr. Ward, post-sutler, waiting for company to go to the States. We rested a few days, I bought a lot of fresh animals, and we started for Independence again. We got along slowly but comfortably. We saw buffalo in innumerable quantities, killed all we wanted, and had some fine sport after them. One of my men, being good at throwing a lariat, caught one while running, but soon found he had not lassoed a cow nor an ox, but a buffalo bull. After throwing the lariat on the buffalo he fastened the other end to the loggerhead of his saddle, as is customary, and jerked his mule. But the buffalo made but little halt, jerking the man and mule heels over head, dragging the mule a few rods, when the lariat came loose, and the buffalo went on as though nothing had happened, with the rope around his neck. This put a stop to catching buffalo with ropes, no one being anxious to repeat the experiment.

We finally got to Independence, men and animals tired out, having been two months and three days making the trip. I delivered the mail, and had to go down the Missouri River to Boonville to telegraph to Washington concerning the return mail, which I had to wait two weeks for. I visited my father-in-law, and then went to the northern part of the State and visited my father and mother, whom I had not seen for ten years; returning to Independence and started the mail for Salt Lake. I here found things boiling against the Mormons. Troops were coming, and great excitement prevailed amongst the people. I had trouble getting the mail or anything else we needed; was threatened strongly, and received the worst kind of abuse from the roughs. Two or three times the trouble came near being serious; but fortunately for somebody, it calmed down without shots or blows. After starting the mail, I went fifty miles up the river to Weston, where I found old acquaintances and friends, had a good sociable time for two weeks, found one of my youngest brothers with a wife and three children, and persuaded them to accompany me to Salt Lake City.

When we got to Laramie, I, with two of my men, started in advance for Salt Lake, changing horses at the different stations, and traveled the entire distance, five hundred miles, in six and a half days, as tired a man as ever you saw. I went to Brigham Young's office and showed my bills of expenditures, and gave a general account of my trip, showing some articles I had published in different papers, rebutting the influences that were going against the people of Utah and the published statement of Judge Drummond, in which I scored him as bad as he had me. I told them that troops would be here; but was laughed at, tantalized, and treated scornfully for making such an assertion. I told them I had been there and ought to know as well as those who sat at home and knew nothing. All hands agreed they were not coming, and Brother Brigham said neither should they come so this ended it.

I had several animals on this express company, had been gone nearly four months, and asked to be excused to attend to my business, which was granted. I went to Green River again, and set up a trading post and ferry. Did very well during the summer; wound up again and come home.

About this time the express company broke up, and all returned home, the mail contract having been taken from them. I lost, on the outfit, about one thousand dollars, besides my time and suffering.

About this time it became well known that a large

number of troops were coming, with Col. Harney at their head. It was "Now, boys, hurrah! They are coming to kill off all the principal men. Old Harney says there are over thirty that he will hang up on sight." This was told over and over for truth. "But," said Brigham Young, "they shall never cross the South Pass; we will stampede their stock and compel them to return." Gen. Burton, with two or three companies, was to do this, and I was to stampede and bring in the stock with a few men that Col. Lander and his surveying party had on Sweet Water, in order to prevent them from getting help from him. All hands were off, I with my party ahead, but could not find Lander's stock. He had them off in the hills ranching. Gen. Burton made several attempts to stampede the stock belonging to the troops, but always found them on the look-out, and returned without an animal.

The troops had by this time got through the South Pass, and the next thing was a general rally of all the forces in Utah, with a determination never to let them come to Bridger. This was in the fall of '57. Troops were sent to Fort Bridger. The post was then, and had been for two years owned by the church, and in possession of Mr. Robinson, who had had charge of the same from the time of its purchase, I having been one of the carriers of the heavy load of gold it took to purchase said place with the stock and goods thereon.

Two or three companies of Mormon troops were sent to this post with instructions to annoy and cripple the enemy by driving off stock, burning trains, etc., so they

Hickman delivering the murdered man Yates' money to Brigham Young to be turned over to the Church. Page 126.

would have to stop; but had orders not to kill unless it could not be avoided in performing the aforesaid orders. The United States troops crossed Green River and came on to Ham's Fork, some twenty miles west. About this time the Mormon troops were seen in every direction making hostile movements. Col. Alexander, then commander of the United States troops, learned what opposition he had to meet, and that the pass down Echo Cañon was well fortified, and several thousand troops at the fortifications which they had made in the cañon. The Colonel then concluded to take a circuituous route, and come into Salt Lake Valley on the north, where he would have an open country. Leaving many supply trains behind he started, but had not gone more than twenty-five miles when Capt. Lot. Smith with his company took a provision train of some sixty wagons, carrying from six to eight thousand pounds to the wagon, and burned it. Smith had been gone six or eight days without being heard from, and the commander, Gen. Wells, became uneasy and sent me with a small company to find him and report. A night's travel took us to Green River, and before it was light we were well secreted in the brush. I sent spies out with field-glasses to see if any one was moving about the country. About ten o'clock Smith was seen coming with one of his men wounded, having his thigh-bone shattered by a ball discharged accidently. My spies met him and brought him to our camp where we lay all day. I saw one of the mountaineers, an old acquaintance, and got him to take the wounded man to his camp ten miles down the river.

The soldiers who had been in charge of the burned train all started for Alexander's army, and left the oxen running loose.

Smith did not want to return until he had burned another train. I left after dark, gathering all the oxen I could find—about two hundred and seventy-five—for Bridger, and got there the next day at noon in the midst of shouts and hurrahs. Smith went back about twenty miles, found and burned another train, and then returned to Bridger. Their provision trains after that were guarded, and when all were safe in the United States camp on Ham's Fork, all stock, horses, mules, and cattle were kept under strong guards.

Our troops were to be seen on the hills in every direction, taking good care to keep out of gun-shot. I was sent to the mountaineers to tell them to keep out of the way, for we intended running off all the stock we could, and theirs might be in the way and get run off with the balance. Most of them obeyed, but some did not.

CHAPTER V.

A CHAPTER OF HORRORS.

CAPTURE OF RICHARD YATES—HE IS MURDERED BY HOSEA STOUT AND HICKMAN—HIS MONEY TAKEN BY BRIGHAM YOUNG—HIS PROPERTY BY THE GUERILLAS—MASSACRE OF THE AIKEN PARTY—BRIGHAM SENDS HICKMAN TO "FINISH THE JOB"—HORRIBLE TREACHERY OF BILL KIMBALL AND GEORGE DALTON—MURDER OF BUCK—A HARD WINTER—ENTRANCE OF JOHNSTON'S ARMY AND ESTABLISHMENT OF CAMP FLOYD—HICKMAN BEGINS TO GET SICK OF BRIGHAMISM—MURDER OF DROWN AND ARNOLD—PUBLIC FEELING ON THE SUBJECT—BRIGHAM'S APPROVAL—HICKMAN'S TROUBLE OF MIND—MISGIVINGS ABOUT MORMONISM, OR BRIGHAMISM—"IN TOO DEEP AND MUST GO ON"——BRIGHAM'S FALSE PROPHECIES—HICKMAN BEGINS TO THINK—DOUBT, ANGUISH, TERROR AND THOUGHTS OF FLIGHT.

ONE Yates, a trader that had been in the country before, had returned with five or six thousand dollars' worth of Indian goods, and stopped on Green River. He had several kegs of powder, and a quantity of lead and caps. He was sent to, to purchase his ammunition, but would not sell it without selling his other goods also. He came to Bridger twice, buying beef cattle for the

Government. Both times I went with him beyond all of our troops, to keep him from being hurt. He would trade at the soldier camps, then go to his house on Green River, passing up and down Ham's Fork. We kept watch of the United States camps every day, and if a party attempted to leave we would make a rush for them and run them into camp again. One day they moved up the creek about four miles, and we saw a vacancy between them and their cattle. We made a rush and drove off seven hundred and fifty head, taking all the fat cattle they had, and some mules. Horses and mules were taken several times after this.

About this time it was noised about that Yates had let the soldiers have his ammunition, and that he was acting the spy for them. One of the Conover boys was on a point near Ham's Fork one day, and saw a lone man traveling towards Green River; he got ahead of him, saw he had a good horse, and halted him, intending to take his horse and let him go. But, after learning his name, Yates, he marched him to Bridger, where he was placed in the big stone corral and a guard placed over him. I was not there when he was brought in. I came to Bridger a few days after he was taken. Thinking there would be no particular use for me for a week or two, I concluded to go home and get some fresh horses, and take home three or four of my men that needed rest.

I will here state that the office I held was that of independent captain, amenable to none but the head commanding general or governor, Brigham Young, unless my services were particularly needed, in which case I was under obligations to act in concert with other officers.

When ready to start I was asked to take the prisoner, Yates, to the city with me, and agreed to do so. The men with me were a brother of mine, T. J. Hickman, who had come from the States with me the summer previous, John Flack and Lewis Meacham. There was a common trace-chain on Yates' ankle, fastened with a padlock. He had a fine gold watch and nine hundred dollars in gold, all in twenty-dollar gold pieces. The money was given to me to bring into the city with the prisoner, but the watch was kept, and what became of it I never knew.

We traveled about fifty miles and camped on Yellow Creek. The next morning we traveled about half-way down Echo Cañon to where the general's headquarters were located, and got breakfast. I delivered General Wells some letters, reported myself, and told him who I had along, and asked him what I should do with my prisoner. He said: "He ought to be killed; but take him on; you will probably get an order when you get to Col. Jones' camp"—which was at the mouth of Echo Cañon on Weber River. After breakfast we started for Jones' camp, some twelve miles distant, and when within three or four miles of the camp, we met Joseph A. Young, a son of Brigham's, going, as he said, to the general's camp to take orders. He hailed me (I being behind) and said his father wanted that man Yates killed, and that I would know all about it when I got to Jones' camp.

We got there about sundown, and were met outside by Col. Jones, and cónducted around under the hill, below and just outside of his camp. He had a fire built for us and sent our horses out, under guard, to grass. He then took me aside and told me he had orders when Yates came along to have him used up, and that was why he had taken me outside of his camp. Supper was brought to us, and Yates soon went to sleep on his blankets. Flack and Meacham spread their blankets and soon went to sleep also. I told them to do it, as I would guard the prisoner until I called them. My brother, being a Gentile, had been sent on to the next station, some ten miles ahead, on business. I remained at our camp-fire until eleven or twelve o'clock that night, several coming and chatting with me.

About this time all was still, and everybody supposed to be in their beds. No person was to be seen, when Col. Jones and two others, Hosea Stout and another man whose name I do not recollect, came to my camp-fire and asked if Yates was asleep. I told them he was, upon which his brains were knocked out with an ax. He was covered up with his blankets and left laying. Picks and spades were brought, and a grave dug some three feet deep near the camp by the fire-light, all hands assisting. Flack and Meacham were asleep when the man was killed, but woke up and saw the grave digging. The body was put in and the dirt well packed on it, after which our camp-fire, which consisted of small wood and brush, was moved onto the grave in order to prevent notice of a change of ground.* Our horses were immediately sent for, and we were off before daylight; went to the next station, found my brother, got breakfast, and arrived at Salt Lake that day.

The next day I took the nine hundred dollars, and we all went to headquarters. Flack and I had a talk, as we went, about the money. He said Brigham ought to give that to us as we had already been to more expense than that money amounted to, from horses used up and other losses, and urged me to get it. I told him I would try, saying to him: "You know how much I have been out, and can testify to it, and I think he will give us part of it, anyway."

Soon after dark Flack and I went to Brigham's office. He asked how things were going on out East, and I told him. He asked what had become of Yates? I told him. He then asked if I had got word from him? I told him that I had got his instructions at Jones' camp, and also of the word I had got from his son Jo. He said that was right, and a good thing. I then told him I had nine hundred dollars given me to bring in, that Yates had at the time he was captured. I told him of the expense I had been to during the war, and asked him if I might have part of the money? He gave me a reprimand for asking such a thing, and said it must go towards defraying the expenses of the war. I pulled out the sack containing the money, and he told me to give it to his clerk (I do not remember who he was

See Appendix—E.

now). The money was counted, and we left. This knocked all the Mormonism out of Flack, and he has never had a speck of it in him since—making many observations of this and other things, of hard work, obeying Brigham Young, and never allowed one dollar for all he had done.

In a few days I returned East, and found Yates' goods and all his property had been taken, and stock belonging to him and other mountaineers. Soon afterwards Sydney A. Johnston came to the army, took command, and started for Bridger. We gave way, burned the fort, and fell back to Bear River, forty miles west. At this time all the able-bodied men in the Territory were called out. Fortifications were erected at the mouth of Echo Cañon, and the troops concentrated there, while constant guards were kept circling around Bridger.

Johnston arrived there and took possession of all that was left—a stone fort and corral—and commenced preparations for winter quarters. As soon as this was ascertained, our troops began to be liberated and sent home. Snow fell deep, and finally all went home except a few guards who were left to watch the movements of the United States Army. There was a great lack of goods and groceries in Salt Lake that winter, as the merchant traders were not allowed to come in with their goods as had usually been the case.

After being at home some time, word was sent to me to have my boys look for a man that had got away from a party at what was called the Point of the Mountain, twenty-five miles south of Salt Lake City. Two boys who were living with me went up the river and returned about noon, and two hours later a messenger came from the city and told me I was wanted at Brigham Young's office immediately. I mounted my horse and was in town in an hour, and went to Young's office. He asked me if I "had seen the boys?" I asked him what boys? and he answered, "Geo. Grant and William Kimball." I told him I had not. I then told him I had got word to come to his office, and wished to know what was wanting. He answered: "The boys have made a bad job of trying to put a man out of the way. They all got drunk, bruised up a fellow, and he got away from them at the Point of the Mountain, came back to this city, and is telling all that happened, which is making a big stink." He said I must get him out of the way and use him up. He told me to go and find the boys, meaning Generals Grant and Kimball, they both being acting generals in the Utah militia at that time, and arrange things with them, so as to have him taken care of.

I found them, and they told me O. P. Rockwell, with a party, had made a bad job and wanted help, and I had been sent for to wind it up. Said they: "Did Brigham tell you what was up?" I told them he did, and had sent me to arrange things. They told me they had things fixed; that when the party, to which this man belonged, first came into the Territory, they had all stopped twelve miles north of the city, and remained several weeks in the neighborhood where George Dalton lived; that Dalton was in town, and they had got him to see this man (whose name I never heard, only he was called Buck), and take him home with him, for he had confidence in Dalton. They said Dalton understood it, and they were waiting for me to come and meet him on the road. They then hunted up Dalton, and told him they had things all right now. Dalton was to leave town a little before sundown, and pass the Hot Springs three miles north of the city, and take the lower road on which there was not much travel, and I was to meet him. I was to know his team because both of his horses were white, and he was to drive very fast.

All being arranged, and the sun about an hour high, I got my horse, and the question was then asked how many men I wanted to go with me. I told them I did not want anyone. They said I must have somebody, and I told them then I would take a man that was standing by, by the name of Meacham. They got him a horse, and we went to the place appointed, and just at dark the wagon came. We called to it to halt. The man, Buck, got a shot through the head, and was put across the fence in a ditch. A rag was hung on a brush to know the place.

We returned to the city to Gen. Grant's, as per agreement, and found him at home with Gen. Kimball, O. P. Rockwell, and somebody else whose name I do not recollect now. They asked if all was right, and I told them it was. They got spades, and we all went back, deepened the ditch, put him in and buried him, returned to Grant's, took some whisky, and separated for the night. The next day Kimball and I went to Brigham Young's, told him that Buck was taken care of, and there would be no more stink about his stories. He said he was glad of it. Buck was the last one of the Aiken's party, of whom there has been considerable said.* I never saw any of them but this man, and him I never saw until I saw him in the wagon that evening.

Much was said that winter with regard to Johnston's army coming in. Arming, equipping, and a general preparation for fighting was the sole talk and business. During the winter Col. Kane, from Washington, came to Salt Lake City to assist in settling affairs. He went to Fort Bridger and then to Washington. Brigham Young told the people to gather up and start south, and such another moving was scarce ever seen.

About this time President Buchanan sent Gov. Powell, of Kentucky, and Ben. McCullough to Salt Lake to settle the difficulty. Brigham Young and some twenty-five of the principal men of Utah got together. Some speechifying took place concerning the former treatment of the people. The Governor told us the consequences of further resistance, and promised peace in case of submission. Brigham Young sat and heard all that was said, then got up and said: "Well, boys, we will have to let them come in—it is for the best; but never mind, I will take care of you." I was one of the party.

Johnston came in and camped on the west side of the city, and sent word to Brigham that if he did not come back and occupy his houses, they would be taken possession of by the United States troops. Brigham was

*See Appendix—F.

Killing of McNeal by order of Brigham Young. "Dead men tell no tales." Page 141.

only fifty miles south, in Utah Valley, with the principal portion of the inhabitants of Salt Lake City and the northern part of the Territory, and the word immediately went forth, "Everybody to their homes." General Johnston moved his troops to Cedar Valley, forty miles south of Salt Lake City, and built the place known as Camp Floyd. This was in the spring of 1858. Gov. A. Cummings was appointed to succeed Brigham Young, and new judges and marshal were appointed.

D. R. Eckles, of Indiana, was chief justice, originally a Kentuckian, and a fine clever old gentleman. I did not get acquainted with him for several months after his arrival in the Territory, but after I did I spent many a social evening with him. By writs of *habeas corpus* I got seven or eight persons out of the probate court jurisdiction and placed them before his honor; gained my case every time by the rulings of the court against probate jurisdiction in criminal cases.

Prejudice existed against me in the United States Army in consequence of the well-known course I had taken, and I did not go about them; while others who had lain back and shoved others ahead that had nerve enough to drive off government stock, now came around, saying, "We have done nothing," and got good fat contracts. Much money was lavishly spent, but I got none, and these half-handed Mormon officials would say: "If it were not for such men as Bill Hickman there would be no trouble in our country." It seemed as much as to say: "You have done our fighting and we have no more use for you." I looked at this state of affairs and thought what a fool I had been. I had spent the fall and winter before, used up several head of horses, and spent a couple of thousand dollars; had assisted in driving in one thousand head of cattle, horses, and mules, and had not received one cent for it; and now others were making money, while I was compelled to lay back. I said to myself: "This has to do this time, but I will try to keep my foot out after this."

I had a sociable time with all the merchants and traders; but, they being speculators, I had no chance to make anything with them. I sold one of the sutlers two thousand dollars' worth of beef cattle at a fair figure, and a few horses at a good price, which was the principal business I did that winter.

During this summer a man by the name of Drown, who had left Salt Lake in '51, returned. His common character was not good. He was charged with stealing horses and cattle before he went away, and was threatened with shooting; but, on his return, promised to quit all his bad practices, paid a widow woman two hundred dollars for a horse he had stolen from her before he left, and seemed to be doing right. But this summer he commenced running to Camp Floyd and telling all the bad stories on the Mormons he knew or could invent, so said. I was at Brigham Young's office one day, and a man by the name of Matthews went with me and sat outside of the door while Brigham and myself had a talk, in which Drown's name was mentioned. Young said he was a "bad man, and should be used up," and instructed me to do it, and put a stop to his carrying news and horse-stealing.

After getting through talking with him I came out and started off with Matthews, who said: "I have got you this time, and you have done enough; I heard what Brigham told you, and I will attend to that." I told him to never mind, and maybe the man would be better. That night a party got together to give a serenade to one of the editors (Seth M. Blair) of a newspaper just started, called the *Mountaineer*. Some dozen of us rode down to his house, gave him a few hurras, which were answered by him, and a few short speeches ensued. When we got back into Main Street, we heard Drown had been shot in the thigh also. I knew nothing of how it was done, not knowing Drown was in the city until I heard he was shot. The next day I saw Matthews, who told me he found Drown was in town, got two men and went to the house he was stopping at; knocked at the door, but was refused admittance, when he kicked in the door, shot Drown, and started running around the house, and met a man who he supposed to be Drown, shot at him, and kept on. This happened to be a man by the name of Arnold, a very quiet, unassuming, good old man, who was in the house with Drown, and ran out to see who had done the shooting. The shot took effect in his thigh, from which he afterward died.*

Much has been said about the killing of Drown and Arnold, and it has been laid to me; but these are the

* See Appendix—G.

facts just as they occurred. Were it otherwise I would state it as plainly as I have other things. This being a matter much talked about at times, and as Arnold has boys who feel bad about their father being killed, they may know, if they wish, the truth of the whole affair. No doubt they have and will be told other stories by those that know I have stated the truth, in order to screen themselves and throw censure on me, and lead the boys to believe in their innocence and know-nothingism about the affair, which is no uncommon thing among a certain class. Some time after this I was at Brigham Young's office, and the subject of Drown's death came up. He said he was glad; it was a good thing, and as far as Arnold was concerned, he had no business to be in such company.

That summer Charles Harrison had a horse stolen from Camp Floyd, which he had bought in Salt Lake City. Hearing it was at Ogden, forty miles north, he got me to go with him to prove his horse; he also got William Woodland, and a man by the name of "Cub" Johnson went along. We stayed in Ogden one day, and the next day started back, Johnson getting his brother and wife, who had lived there, in a carriage to bring them to the city. A man by the name of Beatty, or Batey, a Californian, who was staying at Ogden, said he was going to the city, and would overtake us.

When he came up he rode past us to the top of the hill, and Johnson said: "What is that d——d rascal doing here? I will settle with him." I told him to behave himself, and supposed all would be quiet, but on reaching the summit he rode up by Batey's side and slapped him in the face, and Batey slapped him in return. By this time Johnson had his pistol out and shot him. He, however, knocked the pistol down and the shot struck him in the hip. Batey drew his pistol, and Johnson knocked it down as he fired, and it took no effect. Batey then put spurs to his horse and rode off some twenty or thirty steps and turned around, facing Johnson, upon which Johnson shot him dead.

The people living near by were notified of it, and Batey's body was taken to Farmington, eighteen miles north of the city, and Johnson was arraigned before the probate court. It was made to appear that Batey had said something to Johnson's brother's wife that was not right, and Johnson secured his acquittal by giving the county prosecuting attorney a twenty-dollar piece.* Some of the stand-ups are even now, while lying seems to be piled up as a fortification for others, saying I killed Batey and took his watch, and this because I got a watch from Harrison, who I was with at the time of the murder. I got two gold watches from Harrison, and then he left the country owing me three hundred and fifty dollars. The evidence is in the county if the grand jury wish to look up the case.

I do not state this as anything of my affair; but as I am giving everything of note that came under my observation, give this. * * * *

---

* See Appendix—H.

BY THE EDITOR.

At this point Hickman gives a voluminous account of his doubts of Brigham Young, the beginning of his skepticism and consequent trouble, which I compress to a few points.

He had been a wild, hard boy in Missouri, had married very young, and joined the Methodist Church soon after; by nature an enthusiast, all the wild energy of his character found vent in the emotional exercises of that sect, and in hot controversy and theological debate. Those observant of religious vagaries in men of more fervor than judgment will not wonder that he reacted from that extreme to the extreme of a hard literalism in Bible doctrine; that his fancy was caught and his judgment captivated by the glorious vision of the Ancient Church restored, with prophets, apostles, and "living oracles" of the Hebrew Jehovah, repeating in the wilds of America all that wonderful story of a gathered Israel fighting its way to a promised land. Many minds will sympathize with this feeling. Of uncultivated conscientiousness and terrible earnestness, he had just enough misguided enthusiasm to easily believe himself one of "God's ministers to smite the enemies of Zion." The Old Testament, the vantage-ground of Mormonism, when taken as our rule of faith, abounds in bloody examples, which this kind of literalism easily turns into bloody teachings; polygamy is not half so easily proved, therefrom, as "blood atonement." The young men of Israel served God by shedding the blood of His enemies. A part of the congregation rebelled, the adherents of

Moses massacred them; a few thousand took idolatrous wives, and their brethren slaughtered them; Sisera tyrannized over God's people, and Jael killed him; Athalia usurped the government, the high priest had her slain; Eglon set up a despotism, and Ehud stabbed him.

From these records Mormonism draws the inspiration of its doctrines—polygamy along with the rest. Then all the native earnestness of Hickman turned to religious fanaticism: anything was "God's service" which "built up the kingdom"; anyone who stood in the way was an enemy of God; Brigham was the "mouth-piece of God to this generation," and Hickman was to obey his orders even to smiting all who would "hinder the march of Israel." But there came a time when he could no longer believe so implicitly. His first doubts, by his statement, were caused by the numerous prophecies uttered by Brigham before the Mormon War, every one of which proved untrue. It is a singular fact that in the Mormon journals themselves are found scores of predictions and statements by Brigham which have been utterly falsified. Besides, Hickman got to know him too well. "Familiarity breeds contempt," even with a prophet. There are so many petty meannesses in the business management of Brigham Young, and so many social errors and acts of personal injustice in intercourse with others, that a majority of those who know him most intimately are apostates.

Often when Hickman was reporting to him, he pronounced persons guilty of certain crimes of which Hickman, from his better knowledge of the facts, knew they were innocent. Soon after the foul murder of Hartley, Hickman was thoroughly convinced that he was an innocent man. In his conversation with me, that was the only one of all his crimes to which he referred with horror. Though "seared as with a hot iron," no conscience could sustain that dreadful burden and be at ease. But by this time Hickman had gone too far. He had begun as an executor of lynch law justice, killing men actually guilty of crime. From that he killed those the Church pronounced guilty; then, by a gradation in crime, which all such biographies show to be natural, he killed whomsoever Brigham Young and Orson Hyde told him to; and lastly, so regular is the growth of crime in man, he killed on his own account.

According to his statement, he would gladly have left Utah in 1860 could he have done so with his family; but he knew too much, and before he could safely break with the Church he had fighting of his own to do.

The remaining history of his life is a melancholy record of struggles—against the Church on one side and personal enemies on the other.

CHAPTER VI.

FROM 1858 TO 1865.

MURDER OF FRANKLIN M'NEAL—STEALING GOVERNMENT STOCK—FIGHT WITH THE THIEVES—HUNTINGTON SHOOTS HICKMAN—BARBAROUS SURGERY—ATTEMPT TO KILL HICKMAN—KILLING OF JOE RHODES—HICKMAN'S PROPERTY "CONFISCATED"—DEPARTURE OF THE ARMY—CAMP FLOYD—GOV. CUMMING LEAVES—GOV. DAWSON ARRIVES—HIS FLIGHT—OUTRAGE BY THE "MORMON BOYS"—DELIGHT OF THE PEOPLE—MURDER OF THE PRISONERS—JASON LUCE—HICKMAN GOES TO MONTANA—INDIAN TROUBLES—RESCUES A TRAIN—ARRIVAL OF GEN. CONNOR AND GOV. HARDING—CRUEL TREATMENT OF THE MORRISITES—HICKMAN BECOMES GEN. CONNOR'S GUIDE—CONNOR AND HICKMAN INAUGURATE MINING IN UTAH—BRIGHAM YOUNG OFFERS HICKMAN $1,000 TO KILL GEN. CONNOR—HICKMAN IN TROUBLE—HE FLIES TO NEVADA—TERRORS BY THE WAY—FOLLOWED BY THE DANITES, BUT ESCAPES—RETURNS, AND SUFFERS FROM MORMON HOSTILITY.

Winter came on, times were lively, and money plenty. One McNeal, who was arrested in the winter of '57, when he came from Bridger to Salt Lake City, for the purpose of making a living, and kept in custody some three or four months by order of Gov. Brigham Young, instituted a suit before the United States district court against Brigham to the amount of, I think, ten thousand dollars. McNeal came to the city from Camp Floyd during the winter, and word was sent to the boys, as the *killers* were called, to give him a using up. The word was sent around after dark, but McNeal could not be found that night, and the next morning he was off to camp again, and did not return until the next summer. I came to town one afternoon, and heard he was upstairs at Sterritt's tavern, drunk. Darkness came on and we got the chamber-pot taken out of his room, so that he would in all probability come down when he awoke with whisky dead in him. Some five or six were on the look-out for him, and among the number was one Joe Rhodes, not a Mormon, but a cut-throat and a thief, who had had some serious difficulty with McNeal, and was sworn to shoot him, and I thought it best to let him do it. Some three or four were sitting alongside the tavern when he came down, it being dark and no lights in front. Rhodes followed him around the house and shot him in the alley. McNeal shot at Rhodes once, but missed him. McNeal lived until the next day, and died, not knowing who shot him; neither did any other person, except those who sat by the side of the tavern. It made considerable stir, but no detection could be made as to who did it. All passed off, and one day when at Brigham Young's office, he asked me who killed McNeal. I told him, and he said that was a good thing; that dead men tell no tales. The law-suit was not prosecuted any further. At this time there was considerable stock-stealing from the Government, and, in fact, all over the country, from both Gentiles and Mormons. I did all I could to get those whom I knew of, or was acquainted with, to quit and behave themselves; but it seemed to have no effect. I threatened to get after them if they did not stop. Some then quit it, but others continued, and swore it was none of my business. A few of them took thirty head of mules from a Government freighter and started for southern California; got one hundred and fifty miles on their road, when they were overtaken and brought back by Porter Rockwell and others. As the freighter only wanted his mules, the thieves were turned loose. I was accused of finding this out and sending after them, and shortly afterward seven of them caught me in the edge of town and surrounded me, swearing they would shoot me for having them captured. Three pistols were cocked on me. I tried to argue the case with them, but the more I said the worse they raged, until I thought they would shoot me anyhow. The crowd consisted of about half Gentiles and half Mormons. Believing that shooting was about to commence, and seeing no other show but death or desperation, I jerked a revolver from each side of my belt, cocked them as they came out, and, with one in each hand, told them if fight was what they must have, to turn loose; that I was ready for them, and wanted just such a one as they were able to give. I cursed them for cowards and thieves: when they weakened and became quite reasonable. This all passed off, but I could hear of threats being made by them every few days; when

Thieves attempting to kill Hickman—who, with a revolver in each hand—wants "as good a fight as they are able to give."—Page 142.

one day I came to town and met Mr. Gerrish, of the well-known firm of Gilbert & Gerrish, who said: "I was just going to send for you; we had seventeen head of horses and mules taken out of our corral last night." I told him it had been done by some of the Johnson gang, and I would travel around town and see them; that they were a set of rascals, and I would try bribery. I found this Joe Rhodes of whom I have spoken. He denied knowing anything about them. I told him I would give him fifty dollars if he would tell me where they were. He then asked if I would betray him to the others that were concerned in it. I told him I would not. He then told me if I would give him fifty dollars down, and fifty dollars more when the animals were recovered, he would tell me, and I would be sure to get them. I saw Gerrish, and he told me to go ahead and use my own judgment about them. I paid Rhodes the $50; he then told me they were about fifteen miles away on the river, hid in the brush, and would be there until after dark; then they intended running them south and keeping away from the settlements, and so get them through to California. He described the place so that there could be no trouble to find it. Knowing of the antipathy of the gang against me, I sent two men, who found the stock at the place described, and no one with them, and brought them to the owners. The gang was very angry at this, and swore they would kill the man that had betrayed them. Not many days after this, the traitor to his own party, Rhodes, said I had played him, and he unthoughtedly had told me something about the animals, but thought as they were Gentiles I would say nothing about it. This was enough—he never told them that he had done it and got a $100 for doing so. They commenced watching for me, and I for them. One Christmas day following I went to the city, all the time watching this party. I stepped through an alley while waiting for our teams. This was their chance. Some half a dozen of them, well whiskied, met me; only one of my friends seeing them. The only brave man amongst them drew his revolver and attempted to shoot me. I caught his pistol, and would have killed him with my knife, but the scoundrels shouted, "Don't kill him! don't kill him!" and stepped up and took hold of him. I did not want to kill him. I had known him from a boy, and had previously liked him; but these scamps had roped him in, and were shoving him into places where they dare not go. I did not see who all the crowd were, but saw two other revolvers drawn on me. This friend of mine says to them: "Don't shoot; if you do, I will kill you." I let Huntington go, supposing his friends would take care of him, as he was the aggressor, and I had spared his life. I put my knife back in the scabbard, and turned to look for Huntington, when I saw him leveling his revolver on me, not more than ten feet off; I gave my body a swing as he fired, and the ball struck my watch, which was in my pants' pocket, glanced, and struck me in the thigh, went to the bone, and passed around on the side of it. I then drew my pistol; but before I could fire he shot again, and started to run.

I shot him as he ran, in the hip, and the ball passed into his thigh; but he kept running. I followed him up the street and shot at him four times more, but did not hit him. I was taken to a house, and Dr. * * * and another, the two best Mormon surgeons in the city, were sent for. They split the flesh on the inside and outside of my thigh to the bone, hunting the ball, and finally concluded they could not find it, then went away and reported I would die sure. I sent for other physicians, and the next morning when they came to see me, I told them I had no further use for them, as my thigh swelled and inflamed so that ice had to be kept on it most of the time for three weeks. Then Dr. Hobbs, of the U. S. Army, a cousin of my wife, came to see me, bringing with him a board of physicians from Camp Floyd. They examined my leg, and pronounced the surgery which had been performed on me a dirty piece of butchery, and said: "Were it not out of respect to the profession, we would say they had poisoned it." But when it was finally opened, behold! out of it came a dirty green piece of cotton, saturated with something, I do not know what, which the butchers had left in it weeks before! No wonder they were sure I would die, after leaving that in my leg. While in this situation, these thieves continued their threats to make a break into the house where I laid helpless, and make a finish of me. This Rhodes was the one appointed to do that, as was told on the streets. Rhodes had become obnoxious to all but his party of thieves. He got drunk one day, and swore he would finish me before he slept. I had good and trusty men staying with me constantly. Rhodes came, as he had said, and wanted to go into the room where I was, but was told that he could not. He swore he would, drew two revolvers, and swore nobody could hinder him. He started for the door, and Jason Luce ran a bowie-knife through him. He fell on the floor, and never spoke. This was the end of Joe Rhodes. Luce was tried and acquitted.

I lay in the city three months and was given up to die. I finally was hauled home, but was not able to go on crutches for six months, and never expected to get over it, as I have twice come near dying with it since I had the fall before bought a few hundred head of oxen which had hauled freight across the plains. My stock was neglected, and I lost a good number of them while I was lying wounded. There was little attention paid to any violation of law there, unless it was a case that was prosecuted by some of the principal men of the city. This case of mine passed unnoticed by the law; and the general saying was: "It was a pity to have a difficulty amongst our own people."

The summer following—'59—the troops were to move from Camp Floyd, and a sale was made of almost every thing except ammunition, which was destroyed. The property sold very low—flour, by the 100-pound sack, 50 cents; bacon, one-fourth of a cent per pound; whisky, 25 cents per gallon; and other things in proportion. I bought ten wagon-loads. The barracks were sold to those who pulled them down and hauled away the lumber; and there has not been a house in the old barracks for eight or nine years. The little settlement adjoining across the creek, known as the town of Fairfield, is a nice little village, but is called Camp Floyd, which is my present residence, and has been for the last four years, ever since I left my place ten miles south of Salt Lake City. There was rejoicing when the troops left the Territory. They had come here, spent a great quantity of money, and went away without hurting anybody—a victory, of course.

Gov. Cumming left the next spring, '60. The next fall another was appoined—Gov. Dawson—who, after being here a few months, was said to have used some seductive language to a woman in the city, which raised great indignation against him. He became alarmed, and made preparations to leave, and a company of the young roughs were selected to follow him out and give him a beating. Five went ahead to the mail station and awaited his arrival, and when he came they gave him a tremendous beating; it is said he died from the effects. It was known the next day in town, and most of the people rejoiced over the beating the Governor had got.

This continued for several days, until the word had reached the States, which made a terrible stink on the Mormons, about the manner in which they had treated the Government official. The newspapers teemed with Mormon outrages. This changed things, and then Brigham Young on the stand gave the men who had beaten the Governor an awful raking down, and said that they ought to have their throats cut. Two of them were arrested and put in prison, and he forbid any person bailing them out. They went for two more, and they fled, taking with them another man, a friend of theirs. They were followed about seventy-five miles; one of them refused to be taken, and he was shot with a load of buckshot, and only lived a few minutes. The other two were captured and brought to the city, showing no resistance.

They reached the city in the night and were given to the police to put them in prison. While going to the prison they were both shot dead, and the cry was raised that they undertook to get away. That was nonsense. They were both powder-burnt, and one of them was shot in the face. How could that be, and they running? This went down well enough with some; but it was too plain a case with thinking men, and especially those who knew the manner in which those men did such things. A great blow was made as a set-off, how the people killed all who would treat Government officials as these had the Governor—innocence was declared by everybody but the gang who had done it, and three of them were killed, and they said they wished the others to share the same fate. After the other two had been in prison about two months, I went and bailed Jason Luce out. The other got bail in a few days. I then learned all the particulars. Jason told me that he was called on by Bob Golden, who was captain of the police, constable, and deputy sheriff, to go in the country with the others and give the Governor a good beating. Golden said he had his instructions what to have done. Luce went to obey orders, expecting to be protected if any trouble should arise from it, he himself having nothing against the Governor, and did not so much as know him. Luce did not like his treatment, and made a business of telling how the affair was. This got Golden down on him, and from that time it seemed that his destruction was sought.*

These things caused a division in feeling among the people; not open, but there was much private talk about such a course of things, which exists until this day. Many of the thinking better class of the people are disgusted with the abominable course taken by the so-called officials, killing off far better boys than their own or many that roamed the country. But their idea was to kill those they did not like, whether guilty of anything or not, as has been done to hide their own crimes, as well as to vent their spite, regardless of right or wrong. This dirty gang of the so-called police commenced about this time, and have done so well they have been kept in office ever since. I will say more about them when I come to the year of their actions.

There was nothing uncommon transpired in '60-'61 more than every once in a while, somebody being killed —some Mormons and some Gentiles—some, it was said, was for stealing and some for seduction, while some of the greatest scoundrels ran untouched. They were good fellows, counsel-obeying curses, and had their friends.

In the summer of '62 I went to Montana after some Flathead Indian horses I had bought the year before

* See Appendix—I.

of the old mountaineer, Bob Dempsy; and that year the Indians were very bad, killing off several trains that were going to California and Oregon on the route north of Salt Lake. This year there was a great cry of big gold diggings on Salmon River, and a good-sized emigration started to that place. I started in company with two boys from here and six Californians, and fell in with a company of forty from Colorado seventy-five miles north on our road. We organized and traveled together. I was unanimously chosen to take charge of the company. We traveled to Deer-lodge Valley in Montana in peace, had a good, jovial set of men and no difficulty. Here we learned that the Salmon River diggings, where the gold was, was four hundred miles further off! Several hundred were alike fooled: some went one way and some another, while about one-third commenced prospecting in that country for gold. We organized in three companies, twenty or thirty in a company, to go in different directions. The company I was in found gold in different places, but not in paying quantities.

I got my horses of Dempsey, and concluded to return home; got on my road, prospecting along the way, when word came that gold had been found in great quantities where East Bannack City now is. I wanted to stop and work awhile, but could not prevail on the five men that were going to Salt Lake to wait; and not knowing any other company going that fall, I concluded to go with them. Provisions were scarce, and none nearer than four hundred miles; some were entirely out then, and wished themselves away. Two came to me to know if I would not take them home with me—both poor men. One went by the name of Dutch John, and the other Irish Ned. Dutch John got a saddle, but poor Ned could find none he could buy. I felt sorry; the Indians being so bad that we thought it entirely unsafe to travel with wagons, so I had to leave Ned; but gave him my claim, tools, and fifteen or twenty days' provisions, telling him that was all I could do for him.

But here I must tell the good luck of Ned and my bad luck. The next summer Ned went to the States with $42,000 that he took out of the claim I gave him. I got home the fall before with $2,000 worth of Indian horses. Here was the difference of one man in luck and another out of luck.

Companies coming in told us there was no use of our trying to get through, for the Indians would be sure to kill us. But we had started, and all wanted to go ahead. The next morning I saw the signal Indian fires raised on the mountain, which were kept up all day, raising a smoke opposite us as much as a dozen times. We traveled until dark, got our supper, raised a big fire, and left; traveled fifteen or twenty miles, left the road and got into a deep hollow, where we had good grazing for our animals. The next morning we were off again, and so continued until we got to Snake River, building fires and leaving them, the Indians following us all the while. But when we got to Snake River, where we expected to be out of Indian troubles, no one was there. Tents were blown down, and wagon-covers flapping in the air, and everything looked dismal. My company looked down in the mouth. I cheered them up by saying we could whip all the Indians in the mountains. The ferry-boat was across the river. One of my men swam the river, some two hundred yards wide, and brought the boat over. No signs could be seen of any person having been there for many days, and a more gloomy time I had never seen. The Indins had whipped trains where there were eighty men, all armed, and some large trains were all killed off—and we, only seven, all told, with forty-six head of horses and mules, all tired from our hard traveling.

We crossed and struck for the mountain, where we could see all around, and let our animals rest until dark. When we started on again we saw fire-lights, and now the question was, "Indians or whites?" After traveling eighteen miles we got close enough to see that there was plenty of wagons—and began to cheer up, thinking we were safe, and rolled into camp, greatly alarming the people. The Indians had had them corralled four days, two trains together, with the ferrymen. Some of these mountaineers had squaws for wives, and two Indians with them. I was acquainted with the ferry party, but they were as badly scared as the others, knowing the Indians' intentions, and said there were five hundred of them circling their camp, and they were afraid to start. But as soon as it was known I was in camp there was a great shout, "We will get out of here now!" Those that never had seen me would rush up and shake hands, as though there had a deliverer come, sure enough. The brandy kegs that had lain at the bottom of their wagons since they left the Missouri River were raised and handed out to us with as hearty a welcome as ever it was to a deliverer of a nation. This was very acceptable to us, for we were almost worn out, and had had no sleep for four nights. My six men looked astonished, to think we had passed through such danger, and asked me if I had realized it. I told them I had, but had kept quiet, as they were all men I had not seen until in Montana.

Next morning a big meeting was held, and I was unanimously chosen captain, with full power to do anything necessary to take them out of the country. We had one hundred and fifty men. I looked at them and thought that about one-third would be good fighting men, and about one-fourth would not fight at all. One man told me that some of the men said they would not fight. I then called the attention of the company, and a vote was taken that I had full power to enforce all orders that might be disobeyed. Upon which I informed them that I was a stranger to most of them; that I had been informed that there were some in the company who said they would not fight, even if the Indians made an attack upon us. I asked the question, what should be done with such men, if found backing out in time of trouble. The cry was: "Do as you please with them, and we will back you up." Then I gave orders, if any man refused to fight in time of trouble, to shoot him first; and if there were any who persisted in such a course, to let me know, and if we had trouble they should be placed in front, and if they undertook to run or back

Meeting of Hickman and U. S. Deputy Marshal Gilson. See Page 190.

out, we would first kill them, and have no dead weight to carry.

A vote of the company was taken to carry out that order. That was the last of men saying they would not fight. All were on hand at a moment's warning.

We rode out, keeping flanking guards and spies on all the mountain points around. I kept the train and stock snug together, and every man with his rifle on his shoulder. Indians were constantly moving around us in different ways. At night, all the stock that could be was tied, the balance was kept in the corral made with our wagons, and a double guard of sixteen men on all the time. We moved on finely until we got to the Bannack Mountain. Here we had to double teams; but only moved a short distance at a time—kept close together, with our spies on all the points around. Just as the last wagon had reached the summit, I saw a smoke rising at the foot of the mountain below us. I saw through my opera-glass Indians coming from all directions, and before we were out of sight there were several hundred gathered at the foot of the mountain where the smoke had been raised. We kept out flanking guards, while passing through the mountain, some five or six miles. We then got into the head of Malad Valley, where we had an open country to travel in to the settlement on Bear River. The Indians gave up the chase, and did not follow us any farther. Two years after this, Gen. Connor having subdued these murderous Indians, I saw one that I had known on Green River some eight years before. I asked him if he had been one of the bad Indians murdering the whites two years before, and he said: "We did not kill you or your party." He then told me that five hundred of them had corralled two trains and the ferrymen, and that I had got to them when they did not know it. He told me he saw me the morning after I had got into their camp, but did not know who I was; but watched our movement, and soon found that a good captain had got amongst them. They could see no chance to run off stock or take the train, and became satisfied that some great war chief was with them. He said the morning that we crossed the Bannack Mountain, he got into the rocks and covered himself up, only leaving a little hole to see out of, that he might see who that big captain was, and saw it was me. He said he went to the foot of the mountain and raised that smoke we saw for the Indians to gather, and when they all had come, he told them that I was the captain, and they then concluded it was no use to try any longer, for I was a medicine man, and a great war chief. I thought he might be telling the truth, and he might not; at any rate I would not like to have trusted any of them at that time.

We reached the settlements in good shape, and I went on home, seventy miles farther, and found everything right, and was aiming to live at home and be quiet, attend to farm stock, and raise my family in peace—not ever intending to again occupy any position in the Church, or as an officer. I thrashed my grain, and seldom went to town.

There had been a new governor appointed—Governor Harding, who, when I first came home, was spoken very highly of by the people. But soon the story changed, and he was said to be a bad man. About this time Gen. Connor—then Colonel—came from California with some three or four hundred troops. Much was said about troops coming into the Territory; but it was thought they would stop at Camp Floyd as before, and probably not be any detriment to the people. Connor had come ahead of his troops, and no person could find out what he was going to do; he never talked beforehand. He went back and met them, and when it was known that he had passed through Camp Floyd, word was sent to him by the head men that he would not be allowed to cross the Jordan River, which he had to do to get to Salt Lake City. But this did not stop him; he kept up his march, crossed the river, and encamped within eight miles of the city. A delegation was sent to him to apologize, or rather deny any such word being sent to him by Mormon authority. The next day he passed through the city and on to the bench, and halted his troops, and established Camp Douglas, which he afterwards built up mostly as it now stands.

The Indians, who had been killing the emigrants for the last two years, had gathered near the north settlements, about one hundred and twenty-five miles north of Salt Lake City. The General sent scouts to seek out their situation, and the Indians sent him word to come on—they were ready, and could whip all his soldiers. The General went with a portion of his men in the winter weather, very cold. His men—most of them—waded Bear River, and found the savages in a deep ravine running across Bear River Valley, where it was smooth and clear of knolls or brush, and he had to attack them while in this entrenchment. He had a two hours' fight, and killed over four hundred. But few escaped that could be found, except the women and children, who were not hurt, only through mistake. He had sixteen men killed on the battle-field, and about as many wounded; and some of them died after he got back to camp. This, together with what he did the next spring and summer, broke up this murderous band. He got great praise; and he truly deserved it. That band had killed off several trains of California and Oregon emigration—men, women, and children—sparing none. This was the same band of Shoshonees which had been after me and party.

I had not, up to this time, made the acquaintance of Gov. Harding or Gen. Connor. I did not aspire to honors or offices, knowing that it would militate against me to be sociable with them. On two or three occasions I refused to go in the room where they were and be introduced to them. One day I was in the city, at Abel Gilbert's store; I saw the door of the back room open, and Mr. Gilbert and the Governor came out. I started out, knowing that my old friend Gilbert would introduce me, and I did not want to get into notice; but, before I got out of the store, I was called back and introduced to the Governor, who said he had been anxious to see me ever since he had come to the Territory.

I found him a frank, sociable old gentleman, but anxious to hear me talk, and get my views with regard to the rebellion that was then going on in the States, and a general expression of sentiments. I could not avoid talking, and finally told him I was Southern-raised, and owned negroes, but I thought it a shame to have good and honest men slain to gratify hot-headed aspirants. I told him that the honest men of our nation ought to have taken and hanged about 250 of those hot-headed, rampart Southerners, and about as many of those cursed Northern abolitionists, and then put an estimate on the negroes, and make the negro-lovers pay a part, and also make the owners lose a part; then colonize them and keep a standing army of United States troops, to prevent either white men or negroes passing either in or out of their country, upon the penalty of death. The Governor laughed heartily at what he called my original sentiment.

I thought I was through, and was about to start, when he says: "No, I want you to go back with me." I went, and was introduced to Gen. Connor. The next time I went to town, I went, by invitation, and spent the evening with the Governor; he became very much attached to me. He told me the course he had taken, and the lies that had been told on him, and also the threats that had been made against him; and asked me what I thought he had better do. I told him to attend to business, and act in his official position, fearless or regardless of all consequences. He says to me, "Will you stand by me?" I told him I would, and he might depend on me if he had any trouble. Ever after this we were the best of friends; and even after he left here, while Chief Justice of Colorado, he spoke in the highest terms of me in two or three publications he made in the Colorado papers.

The summer previous to this, a sect known as Morrisites arose, and established a church on Weber River, forty miles north of Salt Lake City, under the guidance of one Joseph Morris as their prophet and leader. They sold their possessions owned by them at other places, and gathered to that place to prepare for great blessings that were to be given them from heaven through their prophet. They increased very fast, and were bold in advocating their doctrine. They were peaceable, and ignorant, as a general thing; but had some smart men amongst them, who seemed as steadfast in their belief as those of more ordinary talent. They were hissed and hooted at by those who wanted mischief, and some of them occasionally beaten. Some were arrested under pretense of being guilty of crime, and then would get misused and turned loose.

Finally they made a declaration that they would not be arrested any more for nothing. This was enough. Writs were soon out, and a *posse* under Gen. Burton was sent to arrest all their principal men. He went some six hundred strong, taking with them a few pieces of artillery, and a fight ensued. Some were killed on both sides. Burton, with his men, shot Morris, and one or two of his principal men, after they had taken their place; and it is said that Burton shot a woman also who sauced him. This is the affair for which Burton was indicted in the fall of 1870, and is now on the move to keep out of the officer's hands.*

These people were cruelly treated, and incarcerated in prison to await their trial for resistance to law and for murder. They however got bail, and, I think in February '63 had their trial. The jury being composed of those who were by no means favorably disposed to them, it was a certain thing that they would be sentenced to heavy punishment. The poor creatures were to be pitied; they were as harmless a set of creatures as I ever saw. But the secret of the matter was, Brigham Young wanted them broken up, and it had to be done in some way.

This thing was much talked of, and several of them went to Gov. Harding, seeking redress, and laying their grievances before him. When the court came on to try them, the Governor said he expected executive clemency would be asked in their behalf, and wished me to attend court with him and hear the evidence, so that he might be satisfied in his mind as to their guilt or innocence. I attended court five days, and was myself surprised to hear the flimsy testimony against them. The Governor says to me, with tears rolling down his cheeks like rain, "Have we not heard enough." I told him I thought so, and he says to me, "Why are you so sad this evening? You do not like the manner in which those poor creatures are treated." I told him I felt more like crying over them than persecuting them. He shook me by the

* See Appendix—K.

hand, and said, "I am glad to see those tender feelings you have for suffering humanity; it will all be fixed in time."

The poor fellows, some thirteen of them, were sentenced to the penitentiary from two to fifteen years. Their friends got up a petition for their release, and most of the Gentiles signed it, but very few Mormons attached their names. The Governor asked me if I was going to sign it. I told him I was. He then asked me if I was not afraid of Brigham Young, knowing it was in opposition to his counsel to have any Mormon sign it. I told him no; that "Brigham Young was as afraid of me as I was of him," meaning that we were not afraid of each other. But he has told and published it in the light that Brigham Young was more afraid of me than I was of him. But be this as it may, I would have signed it in the face of all the Brigham Youngs this side of Europe, regardless of all consequences.

Shortly after this, General Connor sent for me—asked me a great many questions about the country, and the mountains, roads, rivers, &c., &c. After getting through, he told me he wanted to hire me as a guide, and might have other business for me to do; that I could stay at home when I was not wanted, but when wanted, would have to furnish my own horse, and be on hand. He wanted me to pilot him to Snake River to see the Indians there, see the country, and go from there to Soda Springs, on Bear River, and locate a military camp for the protection of the emigration. He also wanted to catch a small band of Indians that had been killing the emigrants, that he did not get the winter before.

In the spring he, with two companions of cavalry, set out for Snake River, while one company of infantry with supplies, started to Soda Springs, at which place the General told them he would meet them. I went as guide.

The General got to Snake River, found a good many Indians, and had a talk with them, and they promised to be good: and so they will—when they are dead. They gathered by request that night, and had a big dance. The General sent me with a lieutenant and twenty-five men up Snake River fifty miles, and to strike from there south, to Soda Springs, where I was to meet him. I was to look out for a wagon road, as it would shorten the route fifty miles to the Montana mines, where most of the travel was going that summer. He found a good place on Snake River for a ferry, and then started across the mountains seventy miles without a trail, for Soda Springs. We met a party sent out to escort us in, but we would not have missed the Springs a mile. Then the General sent me with a party down Bear River on the north side, with a lieutenant and a party down the other side to look out the practicability of a wagon road down the river. When we returned, the company of infantry had arrived, and the General had located a military post. I continued in the business of guide, and in the fall following piloted the General to Goose-creek Mountain, some 300 miles northwest of Salt Lake City, and from there to Soda Springs eastward, where he had the spring before stationed a company of troops. He paid off those troops that were there, and sent me with Lieutenant Finnerty to the Snake River ferry to pay off a *posse* of troops, which had been kept there during the summer, for the protection of the ferry and emigration.

We returned, after having paid off the soldiers, to Soda Springs, and started for home on a tremendous cold day. Had a canteen of whisky which we hung up on a bush when we camped. The next morning was as cold as blazes. The lieutenant proposed taking a drink; but no sooner had he filled his mouth than he spat it in the fire, declaring there was sand in it, and said he would give the Commissary hell for putting sand in whisky for him. He poured some in a cup and found it had small particles of ice all through it, which the Lieutenant had mistaken for sand.

General Connor asked me about mines, and said he knew it was not the wish of Brigham Young to have mines opened in this country. He asked me also if I had any scruples about it, on account of what Brigham Young had said—I told him I had not, and afterwards brought him a good piece of Galena ore from Bingham Cañon, which was the start of mining in Utah. Leads were located, work down, and prospecting by different parties continued, many laboring under great disadvantages; but it has continued until now, showing one of the greatest mineral countries in the world. I have located and helped others who have made nice sums of money; but many instances have been neglected, and after putting parties in possession of good leads, with the promise of having a show with them, have had my name scratched off the books, or the lead re-located. Miners, as a general thing, are honest and punctual men; but like all other classes of men, have unprincipled dogs among them.

A goodly number of Gen. Connor's men being Californians and miners, were, when they had nothing else to do, by permission, prospecting the country for precious metals. They made many good discoveries, and organized districts. They located leads in Stockton, the Cottonwoods, Bingham Cañon, East Cañon, and other places; and it can truly be said of the General that he was not only a good general, subduing the hostile Indians, and maintaining his dignity as a commander of the Utah district amidst many brawling outrages of the people of Utah, but was the main developer of the Utah mines against all opposition of the principal men. He in this, like all other business, took his own course quietly along, regarding them as a big dog would the barking of fists, or a locomotive the buzzing of flies.

And here I will state that just before this I had my last break with Brigham Young. In the spring or early summer of 1863 I went in town, and Brigham Young sent for me. When I got to his place he said: "That Gen. Connor is nothing but an Irish ditcher, and don't belong in this country, and you are the man to get him out of it." After some more talk he said: "If I would kidnap Connor and set him over into California, he would attend to the help and give me one thousand dollars, and all expenses paid." I laughed at this, and made no reply. Nobody knew then how I stood, and I did not know how they looked on me. Six months after that Brigham Young repeated his previous conversation with me, and said Connor was a bad man, calculated to do a great deal of injury to this people, and ought to be used up. "Now," said he, "you are the man to do it; you travel with him as pilot and guide, and you could easily do it, and it could be laid to the Indians. You can have a great deal more money than if you had kidnapped him and taken him to California." Then I spoke up to Brigham Young for the first time in my life, and said I would not do it; that General Connor was a good man, and the best officer ever in Utah, and I knew him to be an honorable man; "and what is more," said I, "it shan't be done; I will see to that myself. I will look out for that." I was rash and stirred up, and spoke sharp, which had not been the way with us in talking to Brigham Young.

The second winter I was in the General's company he told me he had lost twelve head of mules from the Government reserve in Rush Valley, and wanted me to hunt them up, as I had done before when animals were lost or stolen. I searched several days, but no trace of them. I returned and made my report to him. He sent me again, saying to me, if any man could find them I could, and wished me spare no pains in hunting. He said I might resort to any stratagem I could, and he would back me up. I was satisfied in my mind who had stolen them, and employed men to assist who I knew they would not mistrust. I soon found where the mules were, and in learning this I soon found out that the same company had been committing burglaries for several months past, and then had in their possession several thousand dollars' worth of stolen goods. I reported to the General. He sent and got the mules. I made known to the Captain of the Police in the city what I had found out about the burglaries, and who had committed them, and where the stolen goods were. He raised a *posse* of the sheriff, policemen, and others, and I accompanied them. We found the goods, arrested the men, and took all to the city. I went home supposing I had done a good deed and would get the reward that was offered for them— three hundred dollars by one man, and two hundred by another. But what did I find when I went to town a few days after? I found the reward-money drawn by their confederates, the police, and a writ in their hands for my arrest, made out on complaint of these burglars with whom the goods were found. I was arrested late in the afternoon, and took a good man with me to go my bail, who swore he was worth thirty thousand, liable to execution. The Probate Judge said it was not sufficient, and I would have to get another worth as much inside of an hour or go to the cells.

Now, this dirty old villain knew I was innocent, but he was a confederate with this well-known clan, the so-called city officials, sheriff, and policemen. A blacker set of scamps I never knew. I got another man who swore he was worth one hundred thousand dollars, liable to execution. I then was reluctantly let go after giving one hundred and thirty thousand dollars bail. This may seem

Pulpit Rock, mouth of Echo Cañon, where Brigham Young preached his first sermon in Utah, and where Yates was murdered by Hickman.

strange, but when you see their motives it will be plain. I was in the Government employ, stood fair with both city and military officials, and all hands had set to break me up, stigmatize, and even kill me for taking the course I did in rendering Government official help.

I had a long trial; but finally got out. They became alarmed, and after I had been in court five days I told the prosecuting attorney that I would give him just one hour to enter a *nolle prosequi* in my case, and write the facts about it and give it to me to be published in the next day's paper, or I would use up his thieving one-horse court with all its theiving officers. The consequences were my request was fully granted, in ample time. These villians from that time to this have sought my life. But I must tell you what they did with their chummies, the burglars; they let them go on promise of some time paying two hundred dollars apiece. It was only a few days after this they were caught in a cellar in the city. The officers having no one to lay their crime upon, they were sent to the penitentiary for three years each, not having done anything only being caught in a cellar where goods were stored away. But when caught with several thousand dollars' worth of stolen goods in their possession, they were released without punishment. This was no uncommon thing for parties who were guilty of great crimes to go unpunished, while those of minor offences were given heavy sentences. This court was a gang that cut and dried many of their cases in the "counsel" before they would come into court, and then carry out their spite upon whom they pleased.

About this time they caught me on a bail bond for two hundred dollars and costs. I had gone bail for the appearance of a man that I knew was not guilty of the charge against him; but when going to Montana, in '62, I delivered him up to the court. They let him loose for some time without any recognizance, and he finally went to California. This old bond, which I had neglected taking up when I delivered up the prisoner, was sued on, after only four years with not a word said about it. But this was the day of vengeance on me, and this corrupt court had all power, and made me pay it with costs, saying, "If he does get money out of the Government, we will try and ease him of all we can."

I had a good stock of cattle—near two hundred head—when I went into the employ of Gen. Connor. I did not dispose of twenty head, and yet, when the war ended and Connor went out of office, I did not have twenty. My friends, or those who should have been my friends, had the good of them. I have been told by good honest people, that they heard their bishop say it was no harm to kill and eat my cattle.

When the cattle were used up, then they commenced on my horses, and in two years I lost about three thousand dollars' worth; and to show that it was all aimed for me, the last raid that was made I had five horses in the portion of the band that was stolen, that I had bought and had not put my brand on them, and they were all turned out of the band, and I found them some thirty miles from home. The balance were run into Nevada; but I did not hear this until it was too late to find them.

Well, what next? I was one of those men who had a plurality of wives, and had children by them all. I had as quiet a family as any one I ever saw of that kind, and what I had done in that matter I had done in all good faith. I had not violated the Congressional law of '62 prohibiting polygamy. Neither did I ever expect to, '58 being the last year I had taken a wife. I felt under obligations to take care of my wives and children; but, to use their own language about me, they seemed determined to use me up. The Bishop and others would say to my wives that I was a bad man, and commenced persuading them to leave me; and they would see that they took their children with them, and I should give them all they would ask. They soon got things going, but never had the pleasure of making me give them a dollar; for I told them to help themselves and take all they wanted. I many times would ask them what I had done, and what was wanted of me? Their reply was, "Oh! you have been with the Gentiles and their dirty Government officers and have betrayed us; it is you that has put Gen. Connor in possession of all the news that has gone to Washington about the Mormons." I would tell them that I had not, and even went so far as to have the General say he had never heard me say anything about the Mormons that would be criminal; but all this seemed to do no good whatever.

About this time, one of Joseph Smith's sons, from Illinois, came to Utah and preached several times, always raking Brigham Young for his misconduct and digression from the principles of Mormonism. The general feeling was very bitter against him. I went to see him, as I told him, out of respect to his father, and we had a general social chat. This was enough: what I had not done before, I had done now, and I was in for what was called "Josephism," and that was enough to damn anybody. I saw I could do nothing in this country, and concluded to leave. I sold my place, farming utensils, &c., repaired my wagons, and got teams ready to start. I was abused by every low dog that came along, for being an apostate. I tried to argue with some about the necessity of my going away under the circumstances, but it was of no use. A great many said they did not blame me, and would go, too, if they were treated as I had been. About the time I was ready to start, I got word from my friends that there was no use of my trying to get out of the Territory with my family and stock, for they were watching the roads, by order of Brigham Young, and I would be certain to be killed.

Then I did not know what to do. I concluded I would go and see Brigham Young. I told him how I was treated, as I had before done. He made very strange of it. He wanted to know by whom. I told him the names of some of them; upon which he sent R. T. Burton, the sheriff, to make inquiry. Of course he knew nothing, he being Brigham's dirty jobber, as he had been for eight or ten years. Brigham Young promised to have things looked to; but when I told him men had been prowling around my house several nights with guns and pistols in hand, he gave me strict orders not to shoot any of them. I begged him to give me the privilege of defending myself; but he said, "You must not hurt any one," the reason being, they were some of his men, and he knew it. He professed great ignorance; but I knew no such raids dare be made without his orders. I talked to him some time, watching him very closely, and finally came to the conclusion that he would call off his dogs, or rather his murderers, and let me alone.

I went home and all was quiet, even those whom I had seen watching my house came round and were very friendly. I still wanted to leave, but seeing the situation of my family—that I would have to leave my children in the hands of those I abhorred, I concluded to round up and live in this country, and see my children raised—hoping and praying that the day would come when I, with my children, could have our rights in this country, and do business for the Government, and be the friend of the Government officers, without losing all of our property, and then have a gang of murderers and robbers always seeking our destruction.

About this time the Sweet-water mines were discovered, and I, in company with others, went to see them, it being in the same portion of the country I had prospected in 1855. I heard when I left home that a company of men had followed me, learning I was going to leave the country. I staid at the mines about a week, the last day I was there in company with one man, I went some ten miles off prospecting, saw Indian signs, and two Indians hiding behind the rocks. We did not go near them, believing they intended hostilities, but kept a good lookout, leaving that place and taking a circuitous route for camp. After we had gone two or three miles we saw about a dozen Indians trying to get around ahead of us, but both being on the best of animals, we soon got out of all danger. I told at camp what I had seen, and that there would be trouble, but could get few to believe it. I then told them I had only a day or two longer to stay, and if they did not go to work and organize, I would start home the next day. There was then about one hundred and fifty men camped in squads up and down the creek, but no organization was gone into. The next morning I, in company with ten others, left for Salt Lake. The next morning the Indians made a raid on their camp, killed three men, and ran off near a hundred head of horses and mules, over half they had. We were overtaken by some of the fleeing party before we got to Green River, a distance of sixty-nine miles.

I returned home, and thought I would get some cheap place, and do the best I could until things would have a change. I bought a small ranching place at the mouth of Bingham Cañon, moved my family and stock there, built a good corral, and commenced to improve. I bought seventy-five head of Spanish horses, and intended to do ranching and stock-raising business. But to my sorrow, I soon saw that I was again watched; men were prowling around day and night, some of Brigham's jobbers. I understood it, knowing his motions so well. I commenced laying out in the brush. I saw two men go into the tent where I was in the habit of sleeping. They had a pistol in each of their hands. This was what I expected, and feared being shot in bed. Two nights after

I saw two men go in the tent again, and two stood outside with guns in their hands. I concluded that there was no use for me to try to live here any longer. The day following I saw one of the party, a man to whom I had done several favors, and I rounded him up and demanded of him what was the cause of this. He agreed to tell me all provided I would not expose him. He said it was not believed I intended to stay in the Territory, and that I was confederate with the United States Judge and Marshal, and was assisting them to knowledge against the Mormons in the murder of Doc. Robinson and others; but if I would go and buy a good farm, and sell off some of those wagons and horses, and make a full showing that I intended staying here, I would be let alone. I would have done this for the sake of seeing my children raised; but seeing there was no truth or honor in Brigham Young, and his promise amounted to nothing, there was but one show left for me, and that was to get away quick, and not be overtaken.

The night before I left, one of my boys, being out, was chased by this same gang, thinking, I suppose, it was me. Now those watching me were men with whom I had never had any difficulty; but were of that kind that would kill father or son at the bidding of Brigham Young. This may seem strange, but there are plenty such in this country, that believe they would be doing God's service to obey, if Brigham told them to kill their own son, or the son to kill the father. For two reasons: One for obeying the great command of Brigham, and having nerve enough to do the deed; another, that the man had done something that his blood should be shed to atone for his sins, and it thereby would be the means of salvation to the murdered man, and honor, and a promise of greater exaltation in the world to come to the slayer. But let me here say that this is all Brigham Young's doctrine; I never heard of any such thing until I had been here several years. Those doctrines of shedding a man's blood to save him,* Adam being God, and several other abominable things of like character, have originated solely from Brigham; obedience to the requirements of the Gospel, as set forth, taught, and understood heretofore by the Mormons, have almost entirely been set aside, and the general teaching is, and has been, to obey Brigham Young's counsel and that of his bishop. Many is the time that at public meetings the people have been taught that the Bible, Testament, and other books of the former Mormon faith were of no use; that those things were good enough in the time of them; but now we had the living oracles with us, and that all divine record was of no more use to us than an old newspaper. Brother Brigham was our Saviour, and would lead us to Heaven; he held the power of salvation for all in his own hands, and had his officers, who administered, such as bishops, etc. The great and all-important teaching to the people is: Obey your bishops, and pay your tithings, and you are sure of being saved. This may seem strange to those who have never heard of such things before; but I assure you there are hundreds in this Territory who are sanguine in this belief

* See Appendix—L.

even now—and as for Mormonism, there is no such thing in this country; it is all Brighamism, and should be called so.

The morning before I left two of those dogs were at my place, very inquisitive about what I was going to do. I told them I was going to conference, and expected to attend every day. This seemed to ease them, and they left. I had also learned that the roads were watched in case I made an attempt to get away. I mounted one of my best horses, and, with a few days' provisions in my saddle-pockets, struck across the mountain west, and did not strike a road for 150 miles. Meanwhile, these special friends called every day to know where I was. The answer was, that I was out hunting my stock; but they smelt the rat, and three men were after me, but were too late. I was not seen on the road until I got to Deep Creek, nearly two hundred miles west, at which place I stayed one night, telling them my business was two hundred miles further, to Austin, to search for some animals that were stolen the spring before. This place was six miles off the line between Utah and Nevada. I knew I was ahead of all the time they could make after me, even if they intended following me; so I took things easy from there to Austin. When I got there I found plenty of acquaintances and friends—the Marshal of the city, Hank Ney, and Benjamin Sanburn, the Sheriff, together with the mail agent, Len. Wines, whom I had known from a boy, Charley Stebbins, and others. I was kindly received and well treated; had an introduction to most of the principal men of the city. I found in the city one mule I had previously lost; had him replevied, and, according to the best information that could be gotten, he, in company with some five or six head of other animals, were brought there by a Salt Laker. After I had been there about two weeks, a man came in town and told me I had been followed to Deep Creek by three policemen; but I had been gone five days when they got there, and they wished him, if he saw me anywhere, to telegraph to them to Salt Lake City. He asked then what charges they had against me, and they told him (he being a Gentile) that I had killed a Gentile close to the city some months before, and that was why they were after me. He told me he knew they were lying, for he had been there himself, and nothing of the kind had occurred. He said they swore if they caught me they would kill me without saying a word to me. They were beaten, and the dirty dog, who is one of Brigham Young's blood-shedders, Sam Bateman, who was in charge of the party who were watching me, made great lamentation, saying he had lost three weeks watching me, and I had got away at last, and would bring great trouble on Brother Brigham.

I got letters from home, in which I was advised to not come back until things took a change. I then concluded to go to California and spend a month or two. I went to San Francisco, found my old and true friend, Gen. Connor, and many other acquaintances; had an introduction to the Governor, and a great many others, and had a good sociable time. I told the General what situation I was in, and got a statement from him, with the signature to it, that I had never at any time made any disclosures to him on Brigham Young, which I sent home.* I then went over the mountain, back into Carson Valley, where my old partner lived that I had mined with in California in '51-'52. I got letters from home saying things had quieted down, and Brigham Young told my son to write for me to come home. But I had made up my mind never to return again, and intended to take shipping from San Francisco to New York, and from there take the cars to Western Missouri, and send for my family.

But just at the time I got ready to start I was taken with typhoid fever; it fell into my lame thigh, and it swelled up as big as a common flour sack. I suffered all that a man could suffer and live. I was reduced to skin and bones, lying on my back for four months, run off from my family, amongst strangers and just alive, for no cause whatever, only the fears of my making statements of Brigham Young's course in Utah. I cannot express my sufferings of both body and mind. Night after night I would lie, scarcely able to turn over, no one to speak to; and was given up to die by every one who saw me for weeks. Language would fail me to begin to tell my feelings. I was innocent of crime, only the obeying of Brigham Young's orders, and would sometimes say, O my God, may the day come when his unjust reign shall have an end!

Finally some of my old acquaintances, Mormon apostates, whom I had befriended while in Utah, came to my

* See Appendix—M.

WASH-A-KIE, Peace Chief of the Shoshone Indians.
See Page 105.

assistance, and took care of me until I got able to help myself. My old mining partner being a bachelor, and about that time taken sick himself, I had to stay with those whom I had never seen. Notwithstanding all this, I continued to take the part of Brigham Young in all conversations, with the exception of talks to a few confidential friends. I was down-hearted and disconsolate, and did not much care what became of me. I concluded to return home and take chances again. I went to Virginia City to take the stage for home, and there found Gov. Durkee—then Governor of Utah—who had been to California, and was on his way home. We procured the same seat in the coach, and had a general chat on Utah affairs. He seemed to know all about my situation, and advised me to take care of myself. He said if it was in his power, such a course of things as was going on in Utah should be stopped; but as he was unable to do anything, he would try and serve out his time quietly, and then leave the Territory.

On reaching home, after resting a few days, which I very much needed, being weak and going on crutches, I, with my wife, went to see Brigham Young. He seemed to express great sorrow for me, made inquiry of the cause of my leaving, and, on my telling him how things had stood, he said I should have come to him. I told him I thought I had said enough to him, and it all seemed to amount nothing. We went to our home where my family had been moved to; some forty-five miles south of Salt Lake City, where they had purchased some houses and lots, and were in a tolerably comfortable situation.

I then commenced looking after my scattered family. I had left three wives at home, besides my first, all living in as much peace as any family of the kind. I found one married to a black Spaniard. This woman had four children, the oldest being a daughter of eleven years. Another wife was just ready to marry, which she did in a few days after I got home. This was all right, as I had, after leaving the fall before, been disfellowshiped from the church. I was then left with two wives—the first and the last—the last having two boys, one six years old and the other four. I was disfellowshiped without any charge being preferred against me, and on inquiry learned it was for going away without permission.

I went to mining, and attended to what stock I had left. I did not find half I had left at home when I started away. I soon heard rumors of trouble on me. I went to see Brigham Young, and wanted to know what charges were against me. I found that the same old thing was up again. I was accused of telling Gen. Connor all I knew, and that the evidence had gone to Washington, and had come out in pamphlet form, and I was the cause of all of it. I reminded him of the letter I had sent him with the General's signature to it. He denied ever seeing such a certificate, and I told him to wait until I could write to San Francisco, and I would have another. I wrote a letter to the General, read it to him, and gave it to one of his clerks to put into the postoffice. I soon got an answer, with the same statements in it that were in the one I had got before. I took it to him; he read it, and says: "Well, may be so." I asked him if there were any other charges against me. He said yes, I had been intimate with the Smith boys, Joseph's sons, of whom I have spoken. I told him I only went to see them out of respect to their father, and never had a private chat with them. This he was not disposed to believe. I went and brought John Smith, cousin to them, who is one of Brigham Young's officials, and had him state that nothing outside of a common conversation took place between us. I asked what more was against me, and he said he did not know. I asked him why I was disfellowshiped. He seemed beat, and was mad, and said, "If it was not right to have done it, it would not have been done," and got up and left. I have not spoken to him but twice since, both times on business. He wanted to know the last time I saw him if I was going to join the Church again. I told him I had for three years tried to find out what was against me, and could not; consequently, I expected to remain as I was. He said he would give me a recommendation to the bishop, and wanted me to be baptized again. I told him that would be an admission of guilt which he and all others had failed to show. "Well, well," says he, "I will fix all that." This was the last of it. I have not seen or spoken to him since. I had no desire to belong to his Church, but would have accepted a re-union for the purpose of having more peace and a better show to do business and raise my children.

Bryant Stringham, the man who took care of what was called church stock, hired me to gather up what stock they had in Cedar Valley, the valley in which I lived. Stringham was a good, honest man, whom I had been acquainted with for more than twenty years. I went at it, got up his wild horses, and traded them off for cattle, and some I sold for money, doing as he had ordered, not charging half as much as others did, thinking when Brigham Young heard it he would be pleased. But to the reverse; he gave Stringham a blowing up, and made him go and advertise that I was not a church agent to gather up stock. Stringham settled with me, like a gentleman; but I could do no business that Brigham Young could prevent. This is only one of several things he hindered me in.

CHAPTER VII.

HICKMAN'S LAST CRIME.

ORGANIZES A MINING DISTRICT—DISAPPOINTED AGAIN—DIFFICULTY ABOUT A PLURAL WIFE—A SPANIARD MARRIES HER AND TAKES THE CHILDREN—SUIT ABOUT THEM IN TOOELE CITY—HICKMAN OUTWITTED—MURDER OF THE SPANIARD—EVIDENCE OF THE CASE—FLIGHT OF HICKMAN—HIS ADVENTURES—KILLING THE MOUNTAIN LION—NEGOTIATIONS OPENED WITH DEPUTY MARSHAL GILSON—HICKMAN GIVES HIMSELF UP—FLACK ARRESTED—THEY TURN STATE'S EVIDENCE—EXPERIENCE AT CAMP DOUGLASS—MENTAL SUFFERINGS, LONELINESS, AND REMORSE—CONCLUSION.

Things kept in a kind of live-along condition with me, not doing much of anything but exploring the country for mines. I found in the vicinity I was living, good indication of minerals, and told the people of my little town that they might have mines near home, and do well if they wished. Many of them were anxious, and wished me to explore for them, and they would do what was right with me for it. I found some leads I thought to be good, and made some locations; after which I drew up laws and organized what is known as the Camp Floyd district, called a meeting, and the laws and constitution, together with the name I had given the district, were adopted. A clerk was appointed and a district formed, and after this I, in company with others, kept prospecting.

During this time I had heard a great deal with regard to the course the Spaniard which married one of my wives while I was west three years previous, was taking. He, not satisfied with taking the woman, was making heavy threats on me, as can be shown by certificate sworn to in Tooele City, of the county in which he lived. The purport was if ever I undertook to take my children away he would kill me; and if ever I came about his place, or he had a chance, he would kill me. I wanted no difficulty with him, and kept away, not daring to go and see my children for fear of serious trouble; but on hearing, and that from a reliable source, a now acting deputy United States marshal, that another low, degraded Greaser was after my oldest daughter, I thought it high time my children should be taken from such a place. To avoid difficulty, instead of going and taking them away as a father ought under such circumstances, I brought a law-suit on a writ of habeas corpus before the probate judge of their county. After all parties were in court, I asked the question of Mr. Greaser and the woman, if they were willing to have the case tried in that court; to which they expressed entire satisfaction, and said they would rather have it tried before the Judge than anybody else. I asked her if she was willing to tell the truth; to which she answered she was, and I had her sworn. She said I had always treated her kindly, and left her plenty when I went away; but she had heard I was not coming back, and thought she had a right to marry.

The court gave me the children, but on their entreaty gave them ten days to deliver them up to me, by their giving bond of five hundred dollars, at the expiration of the time. The Judge, being no good friend of mine and afraid of the Spaniard, assessed the costs of the suit to me. At the expiration of the ten days I sent for my children, giving the man an order for them. They accepted the order, put the children into the wagon, and said to him, "Now we are clear," to which he answered, "Yes." When my man got a little ways, the children jumped out of the wagon and ran back into the house, and told him to drive on. The Greaser had my receipt of delivery, and was all right now.

He and the woman then took my children and ran them to Salt Lake City, to see if they could not institute another suit, and keep the children in spite of me. They were sent back for a transcript from the court, so as to commence another law-suit, leaving the children in Salt Lake City. That night, a little after dark, some person called the Greaser* to the door and put, they say, a dozen buckshot through him, killing him instantly, and his chummy that was after my daughter was shot down, but has gotten well. Some four or five days after this I heard I was accused of it, and in about ten days, as near as I can recollect, I heard there was a writ issued for my arrest on the oath of the woman, who was in a

* See Appendix—N.

second room back, but said she heard my voice outside of the house. From what I could hear she seemed to be willing to swear anything. I got alarmed about it, and concluded to keep out of the way awhile. This was in the fall of '70.

I roamed around in the mountains, sometimes alone and sometimes I had company. I went to the Eastern outside settlements, and concluded to spend a month or two hunting elk and bear. The snow had just begun to drive the game out of the high mountains. I killed some deer and one mountain lion—a very large one—I had a great time in getting him. I tracked him fifteen miles, and saw him lying in some brush on a sunny hillside. I was within fifty steps of him when I first saw him, and he was looking straight at me. I thought the safest way for me was to shoot on my horse. I took aim at his head, and just as I pulled the trigger he raised his head, which caused the shot to pass through his nose just below his eyes; he bounded and scared my horse, which made such a lunge that I had to drop my gun to save myself from falling. Away my horse went with me, but as soon as I could gather the reins I wheeled him around and saw the lion close behind me. He ran against a tree and fell. I drew my revolver and gave him three shots which caused him to stretch out, making the worst roar I ever heard from any wild animal. I sat on my horse for some time to see if he was dead, then got off and was satisfied from examining him that he was blinded from the first shot I gave him.

A few days after I was taken with the typhoid fever,

and, as it served me three years before, it fell into my lame thigh, and in twenty hours it was so swollen that I could not walk. In this situation I remained until I had it lanced, but was not able to walk for two months. I was hauled home, and then to other places until I got well enough to ride around.

During this winter I got word often of Deputy Marshal H. Gilson seeking to see me. When I learned that, I did not think it policy to see him, as I had been informed he was one of the deputies of M. T. Patrick, United States marshal, and could not understand why he wanted to see me, unless it was to arrest me. So I declined to see him. He seemed determined, and called on my son George and told him that if I would consent to see him he would go to any point I might direct without arms, and meet me and my friends armed. This seemed to me fair enough, and I concluded to see him without delay, and told my son to inform him of the fact. He did so, and on the 15th of April, '71, I repaired to his herd-house, in Ferner Valley, sixteen miles west of Nephi, where his brother had a large band of horses.

Not being entirely satisfied about his intentions, I kept my arms in readiness for immediate use if any treachery was intended on his part. I found him in the cabin, about to sit down to his dinner. He arose and came towards me with extended hands, saying: "How do you do? Sit down and partake of such as we have." I became assured in a moment that he did not want to arrest me, and I sat down and partook of his fare. After dinner we took a stroll, and then I found the reason why he had sent for me. He informed me he was a detective, whose purpose it was to find out the real criminals of Utah, that he had been in the work for about eighteen months, and had learned much, and had found out how I had been treated in this country, and that I could give the key-note to all the villainous transactions. He said he could not give me any hope of pardon for the many crimes in which I had participated, further than that he believed, if I made a clean breast of it, it would be greatly in my favor. I informed him I had long wished for the time to come that I might unbosom myself where it would do some good; and I had confidence in him more than any other man that had ever talked to me on the subject.

I asked him whom he was relying on to put the thing through? He told me that R. N. Baskin was the man. This satisfied me, as I knew that Baskin was a man that did not know the word fail; at least, would never give up beaten while there was a chance of success. I found Gilson to be a man that had had much experience in his life in his line, and was well posted on the crimes of Utah. He was conversant on the most prominent cases, and held the correct theory, that the leaders of the Church were the guilty party, and not the laymen. He conversed about many cases with which I was connected; and finally elected the case of Yates as the one on which we could with the greatest safety rely for prosecuting Brigham Young. I then gave him a full statement of the case and the names of the witnesses that would make the circumstances complete.

Gilson is a man about thirty-five years of age, with dark hair, and six feet two in height, and weighs 230 pounds. He is always on the alert, quick of perception, and of a genial and kind disposition: and to him and R. N. Baskin may be largely credited the success of the Federal authority over Mormon terrorism and trickery. But with them alone nothing could have been done. All have done their part—all have done well; and Utah's future can now be seen with her rising sun of prosperity instead of lowering clouds of adversity and misrule.

I told them I had made statements to honorable men years ago what I would do when the time came, that I thought I could do it and not be killed, and have the law enforced so as to accomplish something when I did, and not have to run for my life. Gilson assured me authoritatively that it could be done now, and that I should have every protection that I needed. I then told him whenever I was wanted to come for me and I would submit, and make full statements of facts as they were. On the last of September he came and arrested me and another man by the name of Flack. We were then taken before Chief Justice McKean for examination, which we waived, and were sent to Camp Douglass for safe keeping. After we had been there some two weeks we were taken before the Grand Jury, and I made a full statement of all the crimes committed in this Territory that I knew of—as I have related them in this history—which statement, together with that of Flack's and others, caused the Grand Jury to find indictments against several persons, and it has caused many threats to be made on me.

Several have said if I ever get out of here I will not be privileged to live but a short time; others have tried to get me out of camp under promise of any amount of money I wanted to make my escape; but it was too plain to be seen that I would not get far before I would be cared for in such a manner that I would not tell more stories. I could easily enough have escaped, as I had the privilege of the garrison without guard or being locked up at nights; but even had I believed I could safely make my escape, there was not money enough in Utah to have caused me to do it. I have taken my stand, made my statements, and I intend to stick to it, let the consequences be what they may.

I have written this while I have been under arrest for the Yates' murder, awaiting my trial. I have received the utmost kindness from soldiers and officers of this garrison—all, so far as I know, approbating the course I have taken. Some of them I wish to mention.

Major D. S. Groden, acting captain of 2d Cavalry, Company D, on the 26th of April, '61, entered the United States service. He is a Pennsylvanian by birth, and was appointed in the army from Kansas. He was officer of the day when I first came to this post, and probably more through curiosity than anything else, spent an hour or so in conversation with me. I was assigned to his company of cavalry for rations, where I have, through his kindness, remained ever since. They are a fine set of whole-souled, clever fellows, of whom he is proud, and indeed he well might be of such a clean, man-like looking company. They are proud of their commander, and when in parade their showing is not excelled by any I ever saw. Lieut. Townsend, one of the best shots I ever saw, was officer of the guard a few days after I came to this place, and necessarily we had an interview, after which war and hunting stories ensued. When he was leaving, he said: "I know your situation. I am glad to have made your acquaintance, and hope you will not back down, but will disclose the facts of things that have transpired in Utah, and if you want any help that I can do, call on me." After this he pulls out a $5 bill and says: "Go to the sutlers and get a couple of bottles of brandy and cheer up; you are in a good cause, and all honorable men will stand by you."

I have remained in a kind of solitary and lonely situation for the last four or five years, often meditating on the past, and at no time have I rested with a contented mind. I came here to Utah in all good faith, and obeyed my leader; I got a plurality of wives, as I then thought (yes, so did thousands of my brethren), in all conscience was my right, intending to treat them as wives, and raise up a posterity who I expected would be honorable in society; but what do I find? My wives, through other advices, have left, and my children are, some in Cache Valley, some in Ogden Valley, some on Weber, some in Rush Valley, all of which I might have stopped, and been able to give them a father's care and instructions, had I not been such a man, and afterwards doing business for the Government, as I had a mind, and associating with whom I pleased, instead of keeping still.

I have had ten wives, and have twenty-four children living, six grandchildren, and one little great-grandson, only a year and a half old; though I am now but fifty-six. I had one daughter born when I was eighteen years old, and she had a daughter, and I was a grandfather when I was thirty-six. But my property has mostly been taken, my children scattered and my life sought, and I lonesome and lonely am, and have been, passing my time in this situation. And now only my good old wife, the same girl I told you I courted and married when a boy, sticks to me and owns me.

Tongue cannot express or man imagine some of my feelings in the few past years. Many is the time when the sun would rise I would wish for night; and when night came I would wish to God it was morning. But I dared not say I had been robbed and ruined, and deprived of all that was near and dear to me; I thought it was all I could do to live by keeping still. I would rather have died a dozen deaths than to pass through what I have, if I could only be alive again and see right and justice triumph! Thank God! I think the day has come, and now is, and in justice to myself, my posterity, the living, the dead, and my country, I think it right to come out and show the damnable course pursued by Brigham Young—guilty as I have made myself, and with no excuse to offer except my fanatical belief. Believe me or not, I was sincere.

O my God! if any of my brethren (who used to be anyhow) in Utah think they can break the laws of heaven or this free Government, and Brigham will take care of them, let them come and see me here—a good enough place of the kind—but me, lonely and no show to do anything for my family, and scarred all over my body, lame, and old, and poor, when I was once rich, and hated by man, and my life threatened if I stir away from this post. I have not given this as a confession or a bugbear story, but have given you, in short, a sketch of all the most important transactions that I was personally knowing to. I might go into the detail of family affairs—women in polygamy, property appropriations, thievings, and when, how, and by whom ordered, and the consequences when not ordered, and many other atrocious deeds of murder done by the order of Brigham Young, which I was not witness to—all of which would make a larger book than this. This I have written not for any speculative purposes, as has been the case with many books in which there was very little truth; but no matter what you think now, the day is coming fast—yes, in Utah!—that you will know the things set down in this book for truth.

APPENDIX.

A.

The statement that "no attempt was made to punish Smith's murderers," is a great error; but it is not surprising that Hickman should believe it, as every Mormon in Utah has heard it from the pulpit a thousand times. The priesthood had worked up such a state of feeling in Hancock County, that the law was utterly powerless; and yet they heap execrations upon all the officers of the State and of the United States, because the law did not avenge the Smiths. Governor Ford, and most of the prominent men of the State, used their utmost exertions to bring to justice all parties connected with the assassination, but were defeated by the defects of the jury system—a system which the Mormons had taught their enemies too well how to take advantage of. From Ford's "History of Illinois" I condense his account of the trial of those accused of the murder of the Smiths:—

"About one year after, the apostles abandoned for the present the project of converting the world to the new religion. The missionaries were ordered home, and it was announced that the world had rejected the gospel by the murder of the Prophet and Patriarch. The congregations were regularly called for worship, but instead of expounding the new gospel, the zealous and infuriated preachers now indulged only in curses and strains of abuse of the Gentiles. A sermon was no more than an inflammatory stump-speech, relating to their quarrels with their enemies, and ornamented with an abundance of profanity—curses upon their enemies, upon government, upon all public officers, were now the lessons taught by the elders to inflame their people with the highest degree of spite and malice against all who were not of the Mormon church, or its obsequious tools.

"The Mormons invoked the assistance of Government to take vengence upon the murderers of the Smiths. The anti-Mormons asked the Governor to violate the Constitution which he was sworn to support, by erecting himself into a military despot, and exiling the Mormons. The latter in their newspapers invited the Governor to assume absolute power, by taking summary vengeance on their enemies, by shooting fifty or a hundred of them without judge or jury. Both parties were thoroughly disgusted with constitutional provisions, restraining them from summary vengeance; each was ready to submit to arbitrary power, to the fiat of a dictator, to make me a king for the time being, and abolish both the forms and spirits of free government, if the despotism to be erected upon its ruins could only be wielded for their benefit, and to take vengeance on their enemies.

" * * * * * In this state of the case I applied to General J. J. Hardin, of the State Militia, and to Colonels Baker, Merriman, and Weatherford, who, with my own exertions, succeeded in raising five hundred volunteers. With this little force, under command of General Hardin, I arrived in Hancock County early in October. The malcontents (anti-Mormon mob), abandoned their design, and all the leaders fled to Missouri. The Carthage Greys fled almost in a body, carrying their arms along with them. * * * * We reached Warsaw about noon; that night we were to cross the Mississippi at Churchville and seize three anti-Mormons, for whom we had writs for the murder of the Smiths; but that afternoon Colonel Baker visited the hostile camp, and on his return refused to participate in the expedition, and so advised his friends. There was no authority for compelling men to invade a neighboring State, and for this cause, much to the vexation of myself and others,

APPENDIX. 199

the matter fell through. Colonel Baker had already partly arranged the terms for the accused to surrender. They were to be taken to Quincy for examination, *under a military guard;* were to be admitted to bail, and to a continuation of their trial at the next term of court at Carthage. Upon this two of the accused *come over and surrendered themselves prisoners.*

"I employed able lawyers to hunt up the testimony and prosecute the offenders. A trial was had before Judge Young, in the summer of 1845. The Sheriff and panel of jurors selected by the Mormon Court were set aside 'for prejudice,' a new panel was selected and elisors were appointed for this purpose; but as more than a thousand men had assembled under arms at the Court, to keep away the Mormons and their friends, the jury was made up of these military followers of the Court, who all swore they had not formed or expressed an opinion as to the guilt or innocence of the accused. The Mormons had one principal witness, who was with the troops at Warsaw, had marched with them until they were disbanded, heard their consultations, went before them to Carthage, and saw them murder the Smiths. But before the trial came on they had induced him to become a Mormon; and being much more anxious for the glorification of the Prophet than to avenge his death, the leading Mormons made him publish a pamphlet giving an account of the murder, in which he professed to have seen a bright and shining light descend upon the head of Joe Smith, to strike some of the conspirators with blindness, and that he heard supernatural voices in the air confirming his mission as a Prophet. Having published this in a book he was compelled to swear to it in Court, which of course destroyed the credit of his evidence. Many other witnesses were examined who knew the facts, but under demoralization of faction denied all knowledge of them. The accused were all acquitted.

"The next term the leading Mormons were tried and

acquitted for the destruction of the heretical press. Not being interested in objecting to a Sheriff or jury selected by a Court elected by themselves, they in turn got a favorable jury, determined on acquittal; and yet the Mormon jurors all swore they had formed no opinion as to the guilt or innocence of their accused friends. It appeared that the laws furnished the means of suiting each party with a jury; the Mormons by the regular jury, the Anti-Mormons by objecting to the Sheriff and regular panel. Henceforth no leading man on either side could be arrested without the aid of an army, as the men of one party could not surrender to the other *for fear of being murdered;* no one could be convicted of crime in Hancock; Government was at an end there, and the whole community delivered to the dominion of a frightful anarchy."

Note the result of five years of Mormon rule among Gentiles: the latter, accused of crime, would not surrender to *any* officer, ever to the Governor of the State unless they could be taken to another county *"under a military guard; a thousand armed men* gathered to keep the Mormons from assassinating Gentiles in legal custody, and no man on either side could surrender to the other *"for fear of assassination.*

Just this would be the condition of Utah in two years, if the Mormons had a State Government there under their absolute control, unless, indeed, all the Gentiles abandoned the State in a body.

B.

"With full power to organize the county." This brief hint points to one fact which explains many of the difficulties presented by the Mormon question, viz.: the excessive power of Mormon Probate Courts. Unlike any other Territory or State, in Utah these County Judges were granted by the Legislature complete, civil and criminal jurisdiction, concurrent with the District Courts in all other matters, and *exclusive jurisdiction* in matters of divorce and

alimony. There is good cause for this: the District Judges are appointed at Washington, and are supposed to be supporters of national law; the Probate Judge is simply the leading Bishop or Elder in each county, appointed by the Legislature, which was "counselled," of course, by Brigham Young. This usurpation endured twenty years, until it was overthrown by the decisions of Judges McKean and Hawley. These Probate Judges had power to organize counties, appoint under officers, and do forty other things which sound republicanism condemns, but which all aided to keep power in the hands of the Priesthood. For full exposition of this matter, see *Life in Utah*, Chap. XVI, (New Edition just issued by National Publishing Company of Philadelphia and St. Louis). The editor would not venture on the egotism of a reference to his own work, were it not that the book is extensively distributed, and can easily be obtained in almost any part of the country by those who wish to inquire more particularly into the history of the Mormons, and other points alluded to by Hickman.

C.

In a few brief words Hickman narrates one of the most cruel, causeless, and cold-blooded murders ever perpetrated. Hartley's case is the one most generally known in Utah of all mentioned in this book, and there is scarcely a question of his innocence of any serious fault. Of all the crimes committed by Hickman this one seems to rest most heavy on his conscience. In conversation he strove to avoid it, and at this point his manuscript is heavily blurred and blotted, with frequent erasures, and every evidence of an uncertain hand and hesitating mind, impelled to. yet dreading the narration.

From the various popular accounts in Utah I select that of Hartley's wife, as told to Mrs. Marietta V. Smith, and published in her work, "Fifteen Years among the Mormons." Be it noted that Mrs. Smith's work appeared *fourteen years before Hickman made his confession*, and that three-fourths of her statements as to other matters are proved true by testimony lately developed, and no other corroboration will be required. Mrs. Smith says:

"About that time Jesse T. Hartley came to Salt Lake City. He was a man of education and intelligence, a lawyer. I never heard where he was from, but he was a Gentile, and married soon after a Momon girl named Bullock, which involved at least a *profession* of Mormonism. It was afterwards supposed by some that his aim was to learn the mysteries of the church in order to expose them. At all events the eye of the Prophet was upon him from the first; and he was not long in discovering, through his spies, good grounds for suspicion. Hartley was named by some one unacquainted with that fact as a fit person to be appointed missionary preacher among the Gentiles. As customary in such cases he was proposed in open convention when all the heads of the church were on the stand, and the Prophet rose at once with that air of judicial authority from which those who know him best understand there is to be no appeal, and said, 'This man Hartley is guilty of apostasy. He has been writing to his friends in Oregon against the church, and has attempted to publish us to the world, and should be sent to hell across lots.' This was the end of the matter as to Hartley.

"His friends after this avoided him, and it was under stood that his fate was sealed. He knew that to remain was death, so he left his wife and child and attempted to effect an escape. Not many days after Wiley Norton told us, with a feeling of exultation. that they had made sure of another enemy of the Church. That the bones of Jesse Hartley were in the Cañons, and he was afraid they would be overlooked at the resurrection unless he had better success in pleading in the next world than in this, referring to his practice as a lawyer.

"Nearly a year and a half after this, when on my way to the States, I saw the widow of Jesse Hartley at Green River. She had been a very pretty woman, and was at that time but twenty-two years old. I think she was the most heart-broken human being I have ever seen. She was living with her brother, who kept a ferry there, and he was also a Mormon. We were waiting to be taken over, when I saw a woman with a pale, sad face, dressed in the deepest black, sitting upon the bank alone. The unrelieved picture of woe which she presented excited our curiosity and sympathy. Accompanied by my sister I went to her, and after some delay and the assurance, that although we were Mormons, we were yet women, she told us her brief story without a tear, yet with an expression of hopeless sorrow, which I can never forget.

"It was not until I had suggested to her that perhaps I had also a woe to unburden as the result of my Mormon life, which might have some comparison to her own, that she commenced by saying: 'You may have suffered; and if you have been a Mormon wife you must have known sorrow. But the cruelty of my own lot is, I am sure, without a parallel, even in this land of cruelty. I married Jesse Hartley, knowing he was a Gentile in fact, though he passed for a Mormon; but that made no difference with me, because he was a noble man, and sought only the right. By being my husband he was brought into closer contact with the heads of the Church, and thus was soon enabled to learn of many things he did not approve, and of which I was ignorant, though brought up among the Saints, and which if known to the Gentiles, would have greatly damaged us. I do not understand all he discovered or all he did; but they found he had written against the Church, and he was cut off, and the Prophet required as an atonement for his sins, that he should lay down his life; that he should be sacrificed in the endowment rooms, where such atonement is made. This I never knew until my husband told me; but it is true. They kill those there who have committed sins too great to be atoned for in any other way. (See note on the *blood atonement*. Ed.) The Prophet says if they submit to this, he can save them; otherwise they are lost. Oh! that is horrible. But my husband refused to be sacrificed, and so set out alone for the United States, thinking there might be at least a hope of success. I told him when he left me, and left his child, that he would be killed; and so he was. William Hickman and another Danite shot him in the Cañons; and I have often since been obliged to cook for this man, when he passed this way, knowing all the while he had killed my husband. My child soon followed its father, and I hope to die also; for why should I live? They have brought me here, where I wish to remain rather than to return to Salt Lake, where the murderers of my husband curse the earth, and roll in affluence unpunished.'

"She had finished her sad story, and we were choking down our sobs of pity in silence, when she rose and walked away, wearing the same stony expression of agony as when we first saw her. But this is but one case among a thousand that never will see the light until the dark history of the 'Destroying Angels,' as the Prophet is sometimes pleased to call them, is unveiled."

Let the reader observe the convincing agreement of the two accounts. Those who are still determined to believe nothing but good of Brigham Young, may fix some sort of a theory; that Mrs. Smith and Bill Hickman, who scarcely knew each other by sight, could construct a conspiracy so complete that their evidence would substantially agree, though given at intervals of fourteen years; that Mrs Hartley, *now living in Utah*, merely imagined that her husband was killed by the Church, and that these three witnesses should all be mistaken or willfully false, when agreeing in every particular! But those accustomed to judging the weight of evidence can come to but one conclusion: Jesse Hartley was murdered for apostasy, and the charge of counterfeiting was cooked up to furnish some sort of excuse to those of the Mormons who could not "swallow the strong doctrine of blood-atonement."

D.

A plurality of offices as well as of wives obtains in Utah. The number and variety of offices held by the same man is both curious and amusing; and I have never discovered any particular limitation either in the written laws of Utah or the common custom, to the number allowed to a "good Mormon." When I first went to Salt Lake City, the Robt. T. Burton often mentioned by Hickman, was Collector of Internal Revenue for the Territory, Sheriff of the County, Assessor and Collector of Territorial Taxes, besides being a Bishop in the church, General in the Nauvoo Legion, husband of four wives, and, with no Gentile knows how many duties, as secret policeman and Danite. One man in Fillmore held the offices of County Clerk and Recorder; Town Clerk and Justice of the Peace; Assessor and Collector of Internal Revenue, and *ex-officio* Overseer of the Poor.

All these arrangements trace back to the one cardinal principle: to keep all power consolidated in the hands of the Priesthood.—See *Life in Utah*, pp. 398-400.

E.

Through the indefatigable labors of United States Marshals and detectives, the entire history of Yates has been made known. His wife, residing at present in Nevada and married again, has written to Salt Lake enclosing photographs of the murdered man, taken a short time before his death. She had always supposed he was killed by the Indians. His remains have been disinterred from the spot named by Hickman, and the chain of evidence is complete. Hosea Stout, a Mormon lawyer of considerable prominence, who was arrested for complicity in this murder, and on Hickman's testimony, admits that Yates was killed *as a spy;*

but insists that he was not present and had no knowledge of the transaction; that Yates was delivered to Hickman to be taken to the city, and neither he nor any other officer saw him again.

F.

Of all the cowardly and cold-blooded acts which have made the Mormon Priesthood infamous, this wholesale murder of the Aikin party stands pre-eminent. Second to that of Mountain Meadow only in extent, it even excels it in wanton cruelty, treachery, and violation of every principle of hospitality, that virtue held sacred even by marauding Arabs or wild Indians, by *all* savages except Mormon fanatics. Fourteen years had the blood of these victims cried from the ground before the whole truth was known, and now, with the establishment of national power in Utah, a cloud of witnesses rise, and every incident in the tragedy is fully proved. From the evidence before the grand jury and in possession of the officers, I condense the history of the Aikin party, and their treacherous murder. The party consisted of six men: John Aikin, William Aikin, —— Buck, a man known as "Colonel," and two others whose names the witnesses do not remember. They included a blacksmith, a carpenter, one or two traders, and others whose businss was unknown, but they were supposed to be "sporting men." They left Sacramento early in May, 1857, going eastward to meet Johnston's army, as was supposed. On reaching the Humboldt River they found the Indians very bad, and waited for a train of the Mormons from Carson, who were ordered home about that time. With them they completed the journey. John Pendleton, one of that Mormon party, in his testimony on the case says: "A better lot of boys I never saw. They were kind, polite, and brave; always ready to do anything needed on the road."

The train traveled slowly, so the Aikin party left it a hundred miles out and came ahead, and on reaching Kaysville, twenty-five miles north of Salt Lake City, they were

APPENDIX. 207

all arrested on the charge of being spies for the Government! A few days after Pendleton and party arrived and recognized their horses in the public *Corral.* On inquiry he was told the men had been arrested as spies, to which he replied, "Spies, h—ll! Why, they've come with us all the way—know nothing about the Army." The party in charge answered that they "did not care, they would keep them." The Aikin party had stock, property, and money estimated at $25,000.

They were then taken to the city and confined in a house at the corner of Main and First South Streets. Nothing being proved against them they were told they should be "sent out of the Territory by the Southern route." Four of them started, leaving Buck and one of the unknown men in the city. The party had for an escort, O. P. Rockwell, John Lot, —— Miles, and one other. When they reached Nephi, one hundred miles south, Rockwell informed the Bishop, Bryant, that his orders were to "have the men used up there." Bishop Bryant called a council at once, and the following men were selected to assist: J. Bigler (now a Bishop,) P. Pitchforth, his "first councillor," John Kink, and —— Pickton.

The doomed men were stopping at T. B. Foote's, and some persons in the family afterwards testified to having heard the council that condemned them. The selected murderers, at 11 p. m., started from the Tithing House and got ahead of the Aikins', who did not start till daylight. The latter reached the Sevier River, when Rockwell informed them they could find no other camp that day; they halted, when the other party approached and asked to camp with them, for which permission was granted. The weary men removed their arms and heavy clothing, and were soon lost in sleep—that sleep which for two of them was to have no waking on earth. All seemed fit for their damnable purpose, and yet the murderers hesitated. As near as can be determined, they still feared that all could not be done with perfect secrecy, and determined to use no firearms. With this view the escort and the party from Nephi attacked the sleeping men with clubs and the kingbolts of the wagons. Two died without a struggle. But John Aiken bounded to his feet, but slightly wounded, and sprang into the brush. A shot from the pistol of John Kink laid him senseless. "Colonel" also reached the brush, receiving a shot in the shoulder from Port Rockwell, and believing the whole party had been attacked by banditti, he made his way back to Nephi. With almost superhuman strength he held out during the twenty-five miles, and the first bright rays of a Utah sun showed the man, who twenty-four hours before had left them handsome and vigorous in the pride of manhood, now ghastly pale and drenched with his own blood, staggering feebly along the streets of Nephi. He reached Bishop Foote's, and his story elicited a well-feigned horror.

Meanwhile the murderers had gathered up the other three and thrown them into the river, supposing all to be dead. But John Aiken revived and crawled out on the same side, and hiding in the brush, heard these terrible words:

"Are the damned Gentiles all dead, Port?"

"All but one—the son of a b—— ran."

Supposing himself to be meant, Aikin lay still till the Danites left, then, without hat, coat, or boots, on a November night, the ground covered with snow, he set out for Nephi. Who can imagine the feelings of the man? Unlike "Colonel" he knew too well who the murderers were, and believed himself the only survivor. To return to Nephi offered but slight hope, but it was the only hope, and incredible as it may appear he reached it next day. He sank helpless at the door of the first house he reached, but the words he heard infused new life into him. The woman, afterwards a witness, said to him, "Why, another of you ones got away from the robbers, and is at Brother Foote's."

"Thank God; it is my brother," he said, and started on.

APPENDIX. 209

The citizens tell with wonder that he ran the whole distance, his hair clotted with blood, reeling like a drunken man all the way. It was not his brother, but "Colonel." The meeting of the two at Foote's was too affecting for language to describe. They fell upon each other's necks, clasped their blood-spattered arms around each other, and with mingled tears and sobs kissed and embraced as only men can who together have passed through death. A demon might have shed tears at the sight—but not a Mormon Bishop. The fierce tiger can be lured from his prey, the bear may become civilized, or the hyena be tamed of his lust for human flesh—religious fanaticism alone can triupmh over all tenderness, and make man tenfold more the child of hell than the worst passions of mere physical nature. Even while gazing upon this scene, the implacables were deciding upon their death.

Bishop Bryant came, extracted the balls, dressed the wounds, and advised the men to return, as soon as they were able, to Salt Lake City. A son of Bishop Foote had proved their best friend, and Aikin requested him to take his account in writing of the affair. Aikin began to write it, but was unmanned, and begged young Foote to do it, which he did. That writing, the dying declaration of "Colonel" and John Aiken, is *in existence to-day.*

The murderers had returned, and a new plan was concocted. "Colonel" had saved his pistol and Aikin his watch, a gold one, worth at least $250. When ready to leave they asked the bill, and were informed it was $30. They promised to send it from the city, and were told that "would not do." Aikin then said, "Here is my watch and my partner's pistol—take your choice." *Foote took the pistol.* When he handed it to him, Aikin said, "There, take my best friend. But God knows it will do us no good." Then to his partner, with tears streaming from his eyes, "Prepare for death, Colonel, we will never get out of this valley alive."

According to the main witness, a woman of Nephi, all

regarded them as doomed. They had got four miles on the road, when their driver, a Mormon named Wolff, stopped the wagon near an old cabin; informed them he must water his horses; unhitched them, and moved away. Two men then stepped from the cabin, and fired with double-barreled guns; Aikin and "Colonel" were both shot through the head, and fell dead from the wagon. Their bodies were then loaded with stone and put in one of those "bottomless springs"—so called—common in that part of Utah.

I passed the place in 1869, and heard from a native the whispered rumors about "some bad men that were sunk in that spring." The scenery would seem to shut out all idea of crime, and irresistibly awaken thoughts of heaven. The soft air of Utah is around; above the blue sky smiles as if it were impossible there could be such things as sin or crime; and the neat village of Nephi brightens the plain, as innocently fair as if it had not witnessed a crime as black and dastardly as ever disgraced the annals of the civilized world.

Meanwhile Rockwell and party had reached the city, taken Buck and the other man, and started southward, plying them with liquor. It is probable that Buck only feigned drunkenness; but the other man was insensible by the time they reached the Point of the Mountain. There it was decided to "use them up," and they were attacked with slung-shots and billies. The other man was instantly killed. Buck leaped from the wagon, outran his pursuers, their shots missing him, swam the Jordan, and came down it on the west side. He reached the city and related all that occurred, which created quite a stir. Hickman was then sent for to "finish the job," which he did, as related in the text.

The last of the Aikin party lies in an unmarked grave—even with Hickman's directions it cannot now be found—and for fourteen years their murderers have gone unpunished. The man most guilty is accounted a hero, and even now it appears that justice may be defeated through the mere indifference of Government.

G.

Hickman's account of Drown and Arnold differs very much from the popular account in Utah. Judge Cradlebaugh says that Drown has sued Hickman on a promissory note and obtained a judgment. which led to a quarrel. Nor did I ever hear the charge of horse-stealing before I saw Hickman's manuscript.

But according to the best testimony of the best men who were then members of the Mormon Church, it was not for stealing or any other crime these men were killed, but for apostasy and spiritualism! This may sound ridiculous, but it is a singular fact that there is no other form of apostasy the Mormon Priesthood so fear, hate, and curse, and no kind of mysticism to which apostate Mormons are so prone, as spiritualism. The whole body of the Church seems only to be kept therefrom by constantly hearing from the Priesthood that it is the "doings of the devil," and nothing seems to interest a young and skeptical Mormon so quick as "circles, *seances*, visions, shadowy hands, and conjurations with boxes, "pendulum oracles," *planchette*, and every kind of forbidden and diabolical nonsense.

Drown and Arnold were spiritualists, and were holding a "circle" —or *seance*—with one or two others, when the house was attacked—as testified to by a reliable man who was present.

H.

Like the foregoing this case differs materially from the popular account in Utah. But the case was never fully investigated. The Mormon Legislature has, practically, provided for the shooting of any who attempt the virtue of a woman; and the Mormons boast loud and long that this "killing in defense of virtue" is the glory of their system.

212 APPENDIX.

The idea that woman might be so elevated and educated as to be the best guardian of her own honor, never seems to have entered their heads. Theirs is simply the Asiatic idea modernized: woman *belongs* to man, and it is to punish any infringement on his property; if a man entice away another's horse or cow, punish him acocrding to its value, and as woman is of most value, if he persuade her away, shoot him.

I.

Jason Luce was shot in pursuance of the sentence of law, in Salt Lake City, for the murder of a desperado from Montana. The circumstances were such that many people in Montana petitioned for Luce's pardon. The other had threatened to kill him on sight, and when Luce was in Montana the preceding year, he had narrowly escaped being killed. But just at that time the Priesthood needed a victim, over whom to make a parade of their zeal in defense of visitors, and as Hickman has stated, Luce's "fate was already sealed."

K.

In order to test Hickman's reliability on these matters, I addressed a note of inquiry to Governor Harding—resident at Milan, Indiana—who was Governor of Utah from 1862 to 1864, without repeating any of Hickman's statements, and received in reply the following interesting acount:

Milan, Ind., December 23, 1871.
J. H. Beadle, Esq.:
Dear Sir—Yours of the 16th instant reached me in due time. If I supposed that your object was merely to add to the notoriety of this man and his "Confession," I certainly should decline your request; but in the hope that the whole truth may be elicited in the present legal proceedings in Utah, I willingly comply.
It was late in 1862 that I first met Bill Hickman, at Gilbert's store in Salt Lake City. I had often heard him, by the humbler class of the Mormon people, represented as a very bad man; but never remember hearing his character mentioned by any one "in authority." This term applies to all, from a "ward teacher" to

the "President" himself. The others spoke of Hickman always with bated breath. He was represented to me as one capable of taking a man by the hand, professing to be his friend, and stabbing him to the heart with the other hand. But I never heard any one charge him with being a thief, or liar, or coward. Naturally enough, I scrutinized him very closely, finding him coarse and rough, but very affable; and could not decide whether the animal or intellectual predominated in his looks.

When introduced, Hickman gave my hand a grip which seemed to mean something; and he looked at me closely from head to foot, as if studying my person thoroughly. Not long after I delivered my message to the Utah Legislature, which has been extensively published in the country and become historical. This was the end of my social relations with Brigham Young.

I think that Hickman called three or four times that winter, and took dinner with me. I found on closer acquaintance that I must modify my first views of him. This was caused by the sympathy he expressed for the miserable Morrisites, whose history has no parallel on this continent since the religious bigotry of the seventeenth century.

The substance of their story is as follows, which may be relied on as correct. Joseph Morris had been a faithful follower of Brigham Young for many years, but at length concluded to turn prophet on his own account. He appears to have been a man of some remarkable gifts; at any rate he caused a schism in the Mormon Church, calling after him several bishops and elders, with the laymen, including five hundred rank and file. With him was one Joseph Banks, a Massachusetts man, I believe, well educated. He was the man who made the speech in Salt Lake City at the time of Greeley's visit. There was no great difference in the doctrines of Morris and Brigham, except in one particular: Morris taught that he was the true prophet, "anointed of the Lord," and Brigham that he himself was "God's Anointed." Taking the testimony of both parties, it would be hard to settle the theological muddle, for both claimed to have the "gift of tongues," the power of healing, and "laying on of hands," of "casting out devils," and so on to the end of the chapter. It was but the old story over again: "There is not room in the Roman Empire for *two* Cæsars."

Early in 1862 the Morrisites left the Mormon settlements and "gathered in the name of the Lord" on the banks of Weber River, some forty miles north of the city. They took all their movable property with them, including a large amount of grain. Various charges were made against them, and legal executions followed. Some men they had sent to a distant mill with grain were arrested and kept prisoners. Fines were assessed against them for refusing to drill the Utah militia; some of their cattle were seized on execution, and others stampeded and driven off. Some of them (there is good evidence) found their way to the church corral. This was carried so far, that the last cow of many a poor man was taken, on which they largely depended, and the little children, not able to appreciate the faith of their parents, often went crying and supperless to bed.

This deliberate cruelty of course created great excitement in the camp of the new prophet. As might have been expected, he stepped over the commands of Jesus, and went back to Moses for guidance; and, in retaliation, ordered a raid upon the Mormon stock, and that their owners should be captured and held as hostages, as this, to say the least, seems to have been the primitive way in which such matters were settled. All this would seem food for laughter, if the ending had not been so tragical.

There was one easy way to settle it: to stop the wrongs continually inflicted upon these poor and deluded people. But the "authorities" had other views. No railroad had then opened up the country to outside influence; twelve hundred miles separated Brigham's kingdom from the last belt of civilization, and he was "monarch of all he surveyed." It was somewhat necessary for him to follow legal forms, and writs of *habeas corpus* and warrants were issued by Judge Kinney (Chief Justice), and placed in the hands of Sheriff Robert T. Burton. He called on the acting governor, Secretary Frank Fuller, for an armed *posse;* his request was granted, and he left the city with five hundred armed men and five pieces of artillery. On the way he received volunteers to the number of nearly five hundred more. Many of these joined Burton's forces, as they expressed it, "to see the fun."

They marched to within half a mile of the Morrisite camp, which consisted of a few log-houses, and several others made of willows, interlaced like basket-work, and plastered inside—no more fit for a place of defense than if they had been made of cobwebs. The *posse* took possession of the Morrisite herd, and killed such as they needed for beef, while the boys in charge of it were sent in by Burton with a paper containing a notice to the commander of the besieged that if he did not surrender unconditionally within half an hour, firing would begin. This is the testimony of Burton himself, upon the trial. Burton had placed his cannon in such a position as to rake the camp with a cross-fire.

Morris had called his people to the Bowery, their place of

worship, to decide what they should do. He told them the Lord would reveal their duty, and the whole congregation raised a hymn of their own, hundreds of voices mingling with a wild charm, and producing a spirited effect upon the fanatical minds which can be imagined. Meantime Morris stood with imploring hands and eyes turned heavenward, and Banks stood by, believing the revelation would come in answer to their prayers. Morris encouraged his people, reminding them of the promises, "They who wait on the Lord shall not perish," "One shall chase a thousand, and two put ten thousand to flight."

But no "revelation" came, and as the last hallelujah died away, the sound of a cannon broke upon the melody, but the shot fell short of the camp (some of the Brighamite *posse* testify that it was a blank shot). The next instant another cannon was fired, the shot struck the Bowery, two women fell dead, horribly mangled, and a girl of twelve years had her chin shot away. One of the women who fell had a child in her arms, which, strange to say, was not injured. Unhappily the poor girl did not die. I saw her at my office afterwards, the most ghastly human face my eyes ever beheld.

All this time the doomed prophet stood looking up to the heavens, as if he expected them to open, and troops of angels descend with flaming swords to deliver him and his people from the hands of the spoiler.

The Morrisites had not more than ninety able-bodied men, all told, with over three hundred women and children. And now commenced assault and repulse, scouting and counterplotting, which continued all night and the next two days. Some ten persons were killed in the camp of the new prophet, and two of the Brighamites had fallen by their sharpshooters. The third day, the besieged being exhausted, a white flag was raised as a signal of surrender. The order was given by Burton for the women and children to separate from the men, which was done, and the latter stacked their arms. Burton rode into camp with one of his officers beside him, and holding his revolver in his hand. He said: "Show him to me." Morris was pointed out, when Burton rode up to him and emptied one chamber of his revolver, the shot taking effect in the prophet's neck. He sank to the earth, mortally wounded. Burton then shouted sneeringly: "There's your prophet—what do you think of him now?" He then turned and discharged a second shot at Joseph Banks, who fell dead. A woman named Bowman ran up and exclaimed: "Oh! you cruel murderer!" Burton fired his third shot, and she fell dead. Morris was meanwhile struggling in the agonies of death, when a Danish woman raised him in her arms, crying bitterly. Burton rode upon her and shot her through the heart, and the spirits of the two victims mingled in one company to that bourne "where the wicked cease from troubling, and the weary are forever at rest."

The *posse* at the same time came into camp, and robbed the houses of all valuables—watches, jewelry, and money—even tearing off the women's finger rings.

The men were marched to the city, and the women taken to different Mormon settlements, after which they roamed about in utter destitution, "scattered and peeled," mere Pariahs of the plains, fleeing from the face of their "brethren in the Lord, and appealing to the Gentile traveler in the name of the merciful Jesus for the pittance of charity.

I soon after arrived in the Territory, and many of these poor creatures came to me, with tears and half reproaches, as if I had permitted it. Many of them were from Denmark, and the poor souls imagined that a governor was a person with almost the prerogative and resources of a king in their fatherland.

March 3d, 1863, was held, under Brigham's management, the mass meeting which "requested" me and the two associate justices, Waite and Drake, to "leave the Territory forthwith." On the evening of the 6th Bill Hickman came to my house and remained late in the night. He assured me that he utterly condemned the action of the meeting, and had many things to say, protesting that he was personally my friend.

It cannot be supposed that I put much confidence in it then, as I knew Hickman was a Mormon in good standing, and I had never heard a word to his discredit by any one "in authority." I am the more particular in reiterating this statement on account of the many charges the Brighamites are now making against him.

He was particularly earnest about the cruelty done the Morrisites, and though pleased to see such humanity in one I had been led to consider so bad, I could not reconcile his previous life with his present conversation. He gave me a short sketch of his life, and did not seem very proud of his title as "Danite Captain." On this subject, however, he was reticent. I asked him how he dared to express such opinions contrary to the wishes of Brigham Young. At the word *dare* his blood seemed to rise. He stopped me and stood up (I often think now of the man and his manner), and said: "Governor, do you ask how I dare do anything that don't please Brigham Young? I *know* Brigham Young and his rabbit-tracks! Rabbit-tracks! I afraid o' Brigham Young! Governor, Brigham Young has more reason to be afraid o' Bill Hickman than Bill Hickman has to be afraid o' Brigham Young." I never looked on a face with more of a scowl of defiance.

He ended by a cordial invitation for me to visit him at his ranche, assuring me that he would make me comfortable. I have no doubt he was sincere in this, though many around me thought differently. I remember one reason he was anxious for me to go was, that I had been a little hard on the personal appearance of some second wives I had seen. Hickman admitted that he would as soon be hanged as compelled to take care of and live with some that he knew; but he assured me he had made better selections. He said: "I want you to see my wives, and see for yourself the *kind of stock* who are the mothers of my children." This small talk may be of interest from the fact that some correspondent, writing from Utah in the interests of those whom Hickman's testimony might damage, says that his character was that of a wife-whipper, and for that reason one of them had fled from him to the Mexican, whom he lately killed.

On another occasion I was sounding Hickman as to Brigham's being a prophet, when he replied: "A prophet! No more a prophet than you or I. Rabbit-tracks! All rabbit-tracks!" Just what that expression means, I cannot say. I then asked: "If he is not a prophet, how is it that you, with more brains than he ever had, allowed such a man to get you in such a position, to the disgrace of yourself and family?" His face showed that he had never faced that question before, and he made no reply.

I learned that he had some knowledge of criminal law, and invited him to attend the trial of the Morrisites before Chief Justice Kinney, to come off in a few days. Fifteen of them were indicted for murder, and sixty for resisting legal process. Each lot was tried in a lump; the first found guilty of the murder in the second degree, and sentenced to the penitentiary from six to fifteen years each, and the others mulcted in fine and costs to more than the value of all their property. They were committed to jail till the fines should be paid. Those condemned to the penitentiary were loaded with ball and chain and put to work on Brigham's road, under the warden, Brigham's brother-in-law. We had attended through the trial, which was nothing but a mockery. Burton admitted his shooting the prisoners, and offered as an excuse that he did not think it safe to let Banks and Morris live. Had I been on the bench I should have had him arrested on a bench-warrant; but it would have been useless. The jurors would all be Mormons, and recognize no law but the commands of "authority." When I asked Hickman at the close what he thought of justice under such circumstances, he denounced in the strongest terms the injustice of the proceedings. In this we fully agreed.

Petitions were gotten up for the unconditional pardon of the Morrisites, which were signed by all the Gentiles, including the two associate justices and the rest of the Federal officials, and all the officers at Camp Douglas. Not a Mormon signed them; but several called at my quarters, always after dark, and by the back way, to say they hoped mercy would be shown the poor creatures; but they dared not let it be known they had taken any part in the matter. Scores of the wives and mothers of the condemned came and fell on their knees and begged with tears and sobs that I would show mercy to their sons and husbands. Many and angry threats were made on the other side in case I favored them, and one Bishop Woolley came to urge me against it, saying he could not answer for my safety in case I pardoned those men. Meanwhile the condemned, who were mulcted in fine and costs, remained in jail, and the others toiled by day on Brigham's road, and came back at night to brief seasons of misery and troubled dreams in their allotted cells.

The petitions came to me at last, too late to be acted on that night. I had sunk to sleep, when a voice was heard outside, calling for the Governor. My son, who slept below, with a six-shooter always in reach, inquired, "Who is there?" The reply came back, "Bill Hickman. Let me in; I have business with the Governor." He was admitted, and spoke: "Governor, did you think Brigham had sent for you when you heard my voice, and was you afraid?" I replied with the slang phrase, "Not enough to do any hurt." He grasped me by the hand, and said: "Governor, I'll bet on you, and you may bet on me." He then stated that he had lain awake that night, thinking about the petitions, and added: "I have been in bed awhile, got up, and rode fourteen miles to sign them. Has any Mormon signed?" I answered that they had not. He called for them, took up a pen, and wrote across both, in letters as large as John Hancock signed to the Declaration, his name—"BILL HICKMAN." Then shoving aside the paper, he said in a confident tone of satisfaction, "There; he can make the most of it. There's one Mormon who does as he pleases for all of him."

The next day I issued the pardon, and soon the Morrisites were united to their now homeless families. Had it not been for the force under General Connor, it is more than probable they and the Governor would have had a hard time. But some mounted mortars at Camp Douglas, commanding the Bee-hive

House and Lion House, made things tolerably smooth on the surface.

Since then I have never seen Hickman. His troubles may be deserved. I would not shield him from the effects inevitable on the perpetration of crime. The rules well settled in criminal law, in relation to approvers, should be strictly applied to him; but it may be that he is able to give facts and data which place his testimony above suspicion. If it prove true that his implication of Brigham Young, Daniel H. Wells, and others, is well founded, and through him the horrid crimes committed in Utah by *somebody*, be brought home to the guilty, he will have done much to atone for his own share in them.

Brigham Young is no fanatic; it is nonsense to say that a man of his coldness, executive ability, and acuteness, can be fooled by such stuff as makes his system. When they talk to me about a man like Brigham believing such fooleries, I can only adopt the saying of Bill Hickman, "All rabbit-tracks! All rabbit-tracks!"

Very respectfully,

STE. S. HARDING.

The editor has many other accounts of the Morrisites, from members of the sect and of the Brighamite *posse*, agreeing substantially with the foregoing.

For more complete particulars as to these and other recusant Mormons, see *Life in Utah*, pages 402-434 inclusive.

L.

"Killing men to save their souls."

This horrible and blasphemous doctrine of "blood-atonement" is not often alluded to now by the Mormon preachers, but is as clearly taught in their former works as any doctrine can be in language, and that it was often acted upon does not admit of a doubt. The theory is simply this: The spirit of the Lord warns the prophet that some men are in a "spirit of apostasy"; to kill them before they commit this sin will save their souls. Others *have* apostatized; to shed their blood will entitle them to a new probation in eternity. See *Journal of Discourses*, Vol. I., pp. 82, 83, 72, and 73; Vol. II., pp. 165-166; Vol. III., pp. 246, 247, 279, 337, 241, 236, 226,

235, and many others. Consider that these sermons were published by *authority of the church*, and are found in their recognized works, and you can appreciate the following, from a sermon by J. M. Grant, in the Tabernacle, March 12, 1854, and recorded in the *Deseret News:*

"The Lord God commanded to not pity the person whom they killed, but to execute the law of God upon persons worthy of death. This should be done by the entire congregation, showing no pity. I wish we were in a situation to keep God's law, without any contaminating influence of Gentile laws; that the people of God might lay the ax to the root of the tree, and hew down every tree that did not bring forth good fruit. * * * * Putting to death the transgressors would exhibit the law of God. * * * Do not traitors to earthly governments forfeit their life? But people will argue that we can try them on, but not for property or life. That makes the devil laugh, etc. See *Life in Utah*, pp. 410-412.

M.

General Connor examined Hickman's manuscript, and verifies all statements in regard to their relations with each other, but did not think it necessary to make a written statement. He resides in Utah, and his coroborative evidnce can be had if desired.

N.

Hickman is careful not to say *he* killed the Mexican. I suspect because he *could not turn State's evidence on that case*. I have no doubt, however, from the evidence, that he was the perpetrator.

O.

As these lines are preparing for the press, the telegraph brings the news that Brigham Young has returned to Salt Lake City, being formally arrested on the indictments for murder, and is now a prisoner in his own house. The pub-

APPENDIX. 221

lic will soon be able, from a judicial examination, to judge more accurately of the truth of this book.

I have in this Appendix submitted to the reader only the most important, and smallest part, of the corroborative evidence. As Utah affairs have been my study for years, a few may desire to know my opinion of Hickman's work. It is briefly this: I am convinced that what he has told is substanitally true; but he has not told *all* the truth. There is good evidence of his having been engaged in other matters of doubtful import, not alluded to in this work, particularly about Nauvoo and in the Mormon march through Iowa. But this evidence is not now at my command in such shape as to present it in convincing form. Many old residents in that section will remember in the work published by E. W. Bonney, of Montarose, Ia., and in old numbers of the Burlington *Hawkeye*, and Warsaw *Signal*, many allusions to Hickman. But the popular verdict will doubtless be that Hickman has confessed enough, in all conscience, and that if each of the other Danites has as much to tell, our worst opinions of Brigham Young have fallen far short of the bloody realty.

THE END.

DOOLY COUNTY LIBRARY
Vienna, Georgia